MAR - - 2000

FOUNT CHRISTIAN THINKERS

Evelyn Underhill

ANN LOADES

Ann Loades is Professor of Divinity in the University of Durham's Theology department. She has edited *Theology* for seven years, in addition to publishing on theodicy, feminist theology and sacramental theology.

The series editor, Dr Peter Vardy, lectures in Philosophy of Religion at Heythrop College, University of London. He is Course Director of the University of London's External BD programme and a former Chair of the Theology Faculty Board. His other books published by Fount Paperbacks are *The Puzzle of God*, *The Puzzle of Evil*, *The Puzzle of Ethics* and *The Puzzle of the Gospels*, and, most recently, *The Puzzle of Sex*.

TITLES IN THE FOUNT CHRISTIAN THINKERS SERIES

AUGUSTINE Richard Price
EVELYN UNDERHILL Ann Loades
FRANCIS & BONAVENTURE Paul Rout
JOHN OF THE CROSS Wilfrid McGreal
KARL RAHNER Karen Kilby
KIERKEGAARD Peter Vardy
LUTHER Hans-Peter Grosshans
SIMONE WEIL Stephen Plant
THOMAS MORE Anne Murphy

EVELYN UNDERHILL

Ann Loades

SERIES EDITOR: PETER VARDY

Fount

An Imprint of HarperCollinsPublishers

Fount Paperbacks is an Imprint of
HarperCollins*Religious*
Part of HarperCollins*Publishers*
77–85 Fulham Palace Road, London W6 8JB

First published in Great Britain
in 1997 by Fount Paperbacks

1 3 5 7 9 10 8 6 4 2

Ann Loades asserts the moral right to be
identified as the author of this work

A catalogue record for this book is
available from the British Library

ISBN 0 00 628026 9

Printed and bound in Great Britain by
Caledonian International Book Manufacturing Ltd, Glasgow

Contents

Abbreviations vii

Date Chart ix

Introduction xi

1 Evelyn Underhill's Life: a Pilgrimage of Hope 1

2 The Way of the Mystics 15

3 Return to the Father's Heart 41

4 Conclusion 59

Suggested Further Reading 63

Index 65

Abbreviations

AB   *Abba. Meditations on the Lord's Prayer*

EM   *The Essentials of Mysticism*

FS   *The Fruits of the Spirit*

G   *Evelyn Underhill*, Dana Greene

GS   *The Golden Sequence*

HS   *The House of the Soul*

I   *Immanence*

L   *The Letters of Evelyn Underhill*

LS   *The Life of the Spirit and the Life of Today*

M   *Mysticism*

MG   *Modern Guide to the Ancient Quest for the Holy*

MS   *The Mystery of Sacrifice*

MW   *The Mystic Way*

PM   *Practical Mysticism*

SC   *The School of Charity*

T   *Theophanies*

W   *Worship*

Details of editions cited are given in Suggested Further Reading

Date Chart

Life of Evelyn Underhill		General Events	
1875	6 December, Evelyn Underhill born		
1907	3 July, marries Hubert Stuart Moore		
1911	Publishes *Mysticism*		
		1914	Outbreak of First World War
		1918	End of First World War
1921	Public Commitment to the Church of England		
1927	Fellow of King's College, London	1933	Hitler seizes power
1936	Publishes *Worship*		
		1939	Outbreak of Second World War
1941	15 June, Evelyn Underhill dies		

Introduction

Evelyn Underhill: writer of 'best-sellers'

Evelyn Underhill had no qualifications and no institutional position such as a job in a church or university which might have been hers had she been a man. She studied, wrote and taught as a lay, married, childless wife of a distinguished lawyer. She struggled through her own pilgrimage to God with the help of a series of male Roman Catholic and Church of England advisers, and shared that pilgrimage with a wide public.

Evelyn Underhill had been introduced to Christianity as a child and as a young woman, but found what she knew of it very unsatisfying. She almost committed herself to the Roman Catholic Church, but balked at it, and left herself 'unchurched' for many years. Finally she found her ecclesiastical homecoming in the church of her baptism and confirmation, the Church of England. In mid-life, more or less at the same time as she became a publicly committed Christian, she took on a semi-professional commitment as a conductor of retreats and adviser to others, even though it was still problematic for a woman to take on such roles.

As she taught and wrote Evelyn Underhill laid bare much of her own inner life. This deeply affectionate and sensitive woman provides us quite by accident with something of a self-portrait. Each of us lives our own life and not that of another, but we can be encouraged by hers, and perhaps learn to live with as much determination and hope as she displays. Her writing is her legacy to us, and the point of this little book is to put her work in context, and to identify some of its most significant features. The single most important conviction of her life is that God extends an invitation to be loved to each and every human being. This is not easy to believe, and she herself endured a considerable internal battle to become fit to respond to this invitation.

Evelyn Underhill's output over a period of some forty years was remarkable. Books, articles, reviews, addresses, essays and letters are evidence of her self-discipline, determination and self-giving. She began as a novelist and poet, but was intellectually and emotionally dissatisfied with what she produced. Her talent simply was not up to expressing her deepest convictions. So her novels and poetry belong to the years of her relative immaturity, and her search for God led her to write in other ways. As she transmitted what she learned in books of various sizes (some of them 'best-sellers'), she contributed to a new wave of interest in the lives and writings of mystics of different cultures and periods. These women and men had lived lives of prayer and adoration of God, whether as solitaries, in the midst of family life, as members of religious communities, or as 'outsiders' incapable of any form of 'domestication' or attachment to institutional organization. Some of them, she discovered, were immensely practical and efficient, thoroughly immersed in the affairs of their day. Between them they exhibited an astonishing variety of vocation and life-styles.

She herself could so easily have enjoyed the self-effacing life of a certain type of scholar, beavering away in libraries, teaming up with friends and acquaintances with expertise in language which outstripped even hers. Evelyn Underhill did not, however, have a merely 'academic' interest in the mystics. She found inspiration in poets, preachers, politicians, soldiers, monastics, mothers and fathers because they spoke with passionate intelligence, enthusiasm and imagination about their experiences of God. She in her turn spoke with the authority of her own religious experiences and convictions, and with the authority of her immense learning. In publishing their writings she both awakened enough interest in them for further scholarly editions and translations of their poetry and prose to follow her own, and transformed herself in the process. As one of her biographers has written, Evelyn Underhill believed that 'mysticism was a way of life, open to all, achieved by the few whose lives were transformed by that which they loved' (G 51). Having discovered this way of life, she taught it to others by every means within her power.

We turn first to a brief account of her life, placing her books in the context of her own pilgrimage. We will look at some of her thinking in two further chapters, and finally a brief assessment of the agenda with which she leaves us will be offered.

Evelyn Underhill's Life:
a Pilgrimage of Hope

Formative Influences

Biographies of Evelyn Underhill almost invariably deliver her, so to speak, new-born into the South Kensington household of a formidably competent barrister father, towards the end of a century in which there had been major changes with respect to the lives of women. Some of these changes may have been of incalculable importance for the course of life she shaped for herself as her father's daughter, and then as the wife of Hubert Stuart Moore, another barrister.

In the nineteenth century there had been major changes to the legal status of married women, who gradually accrued the rights of the unmarried, such as the right to inherit and bequeath property, to sue and to be sued, and to make contracts. In other words, married women gained a legal existence. The campaigns to secure for women the right to vote still had to be fought and won in the twentieth century, however. If we find it almost incomprehensible that universal suffrage should have been fought over so fiercely, it is because we have forgotten that the right to vote had symbolic importance. It indicated that women had minds and wills of their own, even if they were married. If their rationality was in doubt, so was getting access to education at an appropriate level to match their abilities. Education in theology was out of the question for all but a very few. In the United States Elizabeth Cady Stanton's *The Woman's Bible* of 1895 and 1898 revealed that perhaps women were better off without the study of theology, as what was on offer was an amalgam of canon and civil law, of Scripture and tradition, which could, and all too easily did, inculcate in women a sense of their own inferiority. It was very rare indeed for learned women to be honoured by the award of an honorary degree, especially if their work was in a theological field. With this very brief sketch in mind, we may better appreciate how Evelyn Underhill's education prepared her for her own independent work as a Christian thinker.

Of particular importance was her time at the newly opened 'Ladies' department at King's College, London, from 1893. There her study of history and languages laid the foundations for some of her later, impressive work on the 'mystics' of the past. She became able to take full advantage of the help that could be given by specialist friends in the British Museum library and in other libraries, in finding her way through unedited and edited texts, and putting their authors into context. Her study of languages was to be fostered by the many trips to the mainland of Europe which she took as spring holidays with her mother, and she clearly expected the same competence in her readers, working in quotations from a range of authors in their own languages, and often without translation.

In her time at King's she was also introduced to ancient philosophy and learned to philosophize in a certain way, to engage with great sweeping syntheses of thought, thinking on a large scale, relating together apparently disparate subjects and information in a grand manner. And she took to it with style. Both her major books – *Mysticism* of 1911 and *Worship* of 1936 – begin with summaries, organized around a series of topics in a manner worthy of the philosophical habits of the day. In years to come the College made her their first woman Fellow, an academic honour her mother had not lived to see (she had died in 1924), though her father did see the offer of an honorary degree of Doctor of Divinity of Aberdeen in 1938 (he died in 1939, aged 88). Evelyn's visits to Kensington Square (which now houses Heythrop College,

University of London) also enabled her to discover the chapel of Maria Assumpta there, one of the Roman Catholic places of worship which for many years was to draw her out of the Church of England and nourish her in a manner inexplicable to her parents. Some of her closest childhood companions were also unable to understand the impact of this new religious environment. One of these, Hubert Moore, was to become her closest friend by about 1890, then her sweetheart and fiancé, and in 1907 her husband.

Exploring Religion

Hubert Stuart Moore and Evelyn Underhill must have known one another very well indeed by the time they made their decision to marry, when she was 32, and about half-way into her work for *Mysticism*, published in 1911.

When, however, she revealed to her fiancé that she was seriously thinking of becoming a Roman Catholic, he found the thought of her relationship with a priest as a 'confessor' quite intolerable. As it turned out, after their marriage in 1907, Hubert had to learn to live with his Evelyn's needs for 'spiritual advisers' whether he liked it or not. Robert Hugh Benson was an Anglican turned Roman Catholic, and, perhaps inevitably, fascinating to her as one who had made the move to Rome. Friedrich von Hügel was a most formidable man, immensely learned and distinguished and experienced, with whom she probably shared a level of intimacy in the things that mattered so much to her that she could not share either with her father or her husband. A more distant enthusiasm was an Anglican Benedictine convert to the Roman Catholic Church, John Chapman. Finally and fortunately, she found two men within the Church of England, first a member of the Community of the Resurrection, Walter Howard Frere, Bishop of Truro, and then a priest, married and with children, Reginald Somerset Ward. Between them, they steered her towards and then through the vocation she was to find later in life, after she finally committed herself to the Church of England. This vocation turned out in part to be that of a retreat and spiritual adviser or director for fellow Anglicans.

Quite apart from Hubert's real discomfort at the prospect of Evelyn's ever becoming a Roman Catholic, Evelyn herself quailed at it when in 1907, the year of her marriage, the Roman Catholic Church condemned the movement known as Modernism. This movement was made up of those who wanted to bring their Church's tradition into closer relationship with developing new approaches in philosophy, psychology and the sciences. Modernists looked at the present and the future rather than to the origins of Christianity for resources with which the Church might relate itself more effectively to the new world which lay before its members. Evelyn Underhill herself appreciated the importance of what they hoped to achieve, and was true to her own education and upbringing by not submitting to church authority. Since she did not feel able even to attend the Church of England's services for many years, but chose rather to attend those of the Roman Catholic Church, she had to endure living without the nourishment of the sacramental life she had discovered.

The crisis over religion at the time of their marriage brought Evelyn and Hubert closer to one another, but even their rich companionship and a full and busy life shared with one another and their friends could not satisfy her, it seems. Evelyn's eyes had opened to the richness of the buildings and liturgy of the Roman Catholic and Orthodox Churches in holidays in Europe and then back in England. She began to explore the resources of the Christian tradition and to make them her own. For instance, she began to find significance in the figure of Mary the mother of Jesus in relation to her own religious experience and development of a life of prayer. In particular, the image of the *Pietá*, the mother bearing her dead son in her lap, became for Evelyn an image of the state of the human soul at one stage of its journey to the divine, and this image turns up in *Mysticism* (see p. 22). In one of her two collections of poetry, *Immanence* (published in 1912, and dedicated to her father), she wrote of this particular image, finding in the court of heaven 'Maternal Life enthroned, and on her knees / The Son of God, the soul' (I 49). The 'Son' here is for Evelyn the false self, slain for the sake of the renewed, truer self. On the far side of such 'death' lay the new life of intimacy flourishing in the divine love. We turn now to her first major publishing success, that of *Mysticism* of 1911, in which she wrote of religious experience as of supreme human importance. Only union with an all-embracing divine love would bring human beings fulfilment, she believed.

Mysticism: Breadth of Vision

In *Mysticism* Evelyn Underhill argued for the reality of genuine awareness of God. She drew on insights from psychology, from history, from the study of non-Christian religious traditions to argue that it was possible to know that one was being grasped and transformed by divine love. Throughout her life, from this point on, she went on insisting that human beings have something about them which is not accounted for by nature, and cannot be explained by it. For she believed that we inhabit two worlds, one changing and the other unchanging, and that we could reach out towards the truths which lie beyond and above the reason with which we negotiate our way through our present life. As human beings, she believed, we have contact with many levels of reality. It is religious tradition which awakens and fosters our capacity to respond to the reality we acknowledge as divine, as being other than ourselves and our world, but which mysteriously pervades it. And since 'the proof of the pudding is in the eating', she wrote of the importance of attending to the evidence of the actual lives of the mystics. To her, they seemed utterly sane, entirely sober, and full of sheer practical energy. Those human beings who had been captured and transformed by divine love included many who returned to the world of their fellow human beings in service to them. In making this latter point, however, she never allowed her readers to forget her own insistence that they get their priorities right. Hers was no merely 'academic' discussion of mysticism, but a form of advocacy. For she reminded everyone with whom she came in contact that the adoration of God was to come first, and the learning of those religious practices which would help to release the self for a fuller life. Thus even the practice of 'unselfing' was not the primary aim. That aim was to allow oneself to be found in God; and 'unselfing', even slaying one's 'false' self, would in fact make possible the attainment of a life of what Evelyn Underhill called 'undivided zest' (M 210–12).

In her search for material for her book, both she and the friends whose help she enlisted looked for material which was not explicitly Christian. She was 'catholic' in the best sense, of being willing to look to the whole spectrum of human experience of the divine for her examples. And she found examples in plenty, most notably in the lives of those whose affective life was deeply engaged with their search for God. They included lovers, poets, mourners and converts, those for whom the whole search for God was above all things 'an intimate and personal relation, the satisfaction of a deep desire', who would most naturally fall back 'upon imagery drawn largely from the language of earthly passion'. She found kinship among the mystics of a very wide range of cultures, therefore, with the Christian tradition exceptional only in its particular capacity for fostering such satisfaction. The reason for this was to be found in the fact that the Christian religion insists upon the personal aspect of the Godhead. In Christ in particular there was to be found an object of intimacy, devotion and desire. Inevitably, a large number of Christian mystics described their experiences using symbolism focused on the person of Christ himself (M 128).

Mysticism was a major publishing success. By the time she wrote a Preface to the twelfth edition of 1930, she was a public figure, precipitated by her writing, her public commitment to the Church of England and a distinctive role within it, into responsibilities which neither she nor those closest to her could have foreseen.

The 1930 Preface reveals significant theological shifts in her own thinking, although she made but few modifications to the main body of the text itself. She had kept up with all sorts of reading in her eagerness to understand how to distinguish 'the genuine spiritual activities of the psyche' from its other possibilities. Crucially, however, in the theology of her day there had developed a new emphasis on 'Transcendence', that is, a 'growing recognition of the distinctness and independence of the Spiritual Order', that is, of 'grace', the 'given-ness' in all genuinely mystical knowledge. She had become wary of giving too much credit to human aspiration to God, and gave much greater weight to the divine activity in making grace accessible to human beings.

She also made generous acknowledgement of the work of those who had worked on the psychology of prayer and contemplation, not least that of the Benedictines Abbot Chapman and Dom Cuthbert Butler, and the work of those who had produced critical editions of the texts of the mystics. Her greatest debt of course was to von Hügel, whose *Mystical Element of Religion* came out as she worked on *Mysticism*. Serious engagement with von Hügel as her spiritual adviser began in 1921, though the publication of her own book on *Mysticism* began their acquaintance. By that date he was almost seventy years of age, a cosmopolitan lay Roman Catholic, with major books to his credit, regarded by some as the most learned and sane man of his times. He was perhaps Evelyn Underhill's most sensitive and constructive critic from the first publication of *Mysticism* until his death in 1925, quite apart from the help he gave at a time of major transition so far as her own spiritual life was concerned. Between the first edition of *Mysticism* and 1921, however, lay the publication of one deeply controversial book, *The Mystic Way* of 1913, and inevitably, the impact of the First World War. We take the impact of the war on her first.

7

Wartime and Beyond War

During the war, Evelyn Underhill worked in naval intelligence as well as doing what she could for the families of servicemen, no doubt as much as was expected from women comparably placed. As the war dragged on, news of the horrors of the battlefields came home, as did the wrecked bodies of some of its 'survivors'. She began, like others, to experience the sheer fatigue of what seemed to be an unending struggle. Her family knew the grief of losing two male cousins in the conflict. Evelyn Underhill did not know it at the time, but for French soldiers, Thérèse of Lisieux had become their 'saint', although she was not formally canonized until 1925. Thérèse's death from tuberculosis, ulcers and gangrene, and her endurance of her dying was close to their own experience. In view of Evelyn's pacifism in the period of the Second World War, the Preface (dated 12 September 1914) to her *Practical Mysticism* of 1914 makes very uncomfortable reading.

In this Preface, Joan of Arc and Florence Nightingale are given as examples of people who had acted under mystical compulsion. Both of them left the deepest mark upon the military history of France and England. 'Their national value was directly connected with their deep spiritual consciousness: their intensely practical energies were the flowers of a contemplative life.' Mysticism might seem hard to reconcile with much of the human history now being poured red-hot from 'the cauldron of war', but the practice of prayer she describes gave people 'renewed vitality'. Of the mystical character she writes that 'its chief ingredients are courage, singleness of heart and self-control. It is towards the perfecting of these military virtues, not to the production of a pious softness, that the discipline of asceticism is largely directed.' That discipline is 'like the intense effort of vision, the passionate and self-forgetful act of communion, presupposed in all creative art', and 'tension, ardour, are of its essence: it demands the perpetual exercise of industry and courage' (PM 49). If 'usefulness' was to be a

8

criterion, there was something here even for 'the most scientific of social reformers, the most belligerent of politicians, the least sentimental of philanthropists' (PM 99). Convent, factory, study or battlefield, multitude or solitude, sickness or strength – any of these circumstances might be the context for a 'violently practical and affirmative' life, giving scope for 'a limitless activity of will, heart and mind' (PM 102–3).

As we might expect from the Preface to *Practical Mysticism*, John the Baptist and Christ in *The Mystic Way* are also worthy war-time models. She has a caustic comment on 'the platitudinous ethics of modern theology' in comparison with what she finds in John the Baptist as a harbinger of the quality of the Christian life: 'Deliberate choice, deep-seated change, stern detachment, a humble preparation for the great remaking of things, no comfortable compromise, or agreeable trust in a vicarious salvation' (MW 79). Of the figure of Christ himself she writes that at the very core of his being, in a way unhindered at the last analysis by the struggle with vice, stress, turmoil, misery and despair, he confronted in his temptation the awesome range of possible attainments before him. But Christ turns his back on solitude, and continuing 'to breathe the atmosphere of the divine' comes back to handle the stuff of life, and makes the choice of 'self-donation' (MW 85–6). It is his life as Evelyn Underhill understood it, that marks something genuinely new in human spiritual history. Thus, those taking a combatant or a politician's role in the war would, as it were, find an understanding of Christ which might inspire them to greater effort.

Fame and its Impact

By writing as she did, Evelyn Underhill was creating an authoritative presence for herself, and in the period after the First World War, by accepting invitations to speak at conferences, and retreats, emerged into public life from a relatively 'private' domestic world which she deeply and rightly valued. Amongst other things, she began to lecture on the spiritual life and education, and by 1926 had begun to give retreat addresses to clergy. As a mere laywoman she was moving into territory which might properly be thought not to be within her range. Yet as a laywoman, who in mid-life made a new and public commitment to the church of her baptism, and with the widest possible Christian sympathies, she may have had considerable advantages. She could not be accused of belonging to any clerical or theological clique. She had a view of the ministry of women which did not threaten male clergy. She was not publicly committed to any particular programme of Christian social action. Without intending it, she had a long training in 'housing' herself in relation to her tradition, in thinking creatively about it, and in conveying it to others. Above all there were many occasions on which she was the only woman to speak and indeed the only woman present. Her learning commanded respect, and it was, in the end, of immense value to her, in conjunction with the fact that she manifestly spoke of that which she had first-hand, personal knowledge, so far as her teaching of prayer and participation in worship was concerned. Certainly she had very high expectations of the responsibility of the laity for a parish prayer life. What she herself practised, she taught to others.

The year 1920, therefore, saw Evelyn Underhill's life turning in many directions. She was uncertain of her vocation, but had for years given advice about religion to her correspondents. By the time she was thirty, others found her vocation for her. To begin with, she was honoured by a very distinctive invitation. Oxford University had in 1920 admitted women to BA and MA degrees, and a Professor Upton had established an occasional series of lectures in commemoration of his sisters. The Unitarian Manchester College, Oxford invited Evelyn Underhill to give the first series of lectures, and thus it happened that she became the first woman lecturer in religion to appear in the University list of the Oxford Faculty of Theology, with the lectures published as *The Life of the Spirit and the Life of Today* in 1922. These lectures, delivered as a now publicly committed Anglican, again exemplify Evelyn Underhill's willingness to learn from anyone who might shed light on the working of the human psyche, and her extraordinary capacity to relate mystics of other religious traditions to her own. She had become more interested in institutional forms of Christianity, however, and she was more than willing to look at the whole range, including General Booth and the Salvation Army. And the vigour of her earlier approach to religious life continued. Evelyn Underhill wanted people to be taught not the weak and sinful things they are, 'but the living and radiant things which they can become'. And she had a tart and perceptive comment to make about the sort of hymns which encourage what she called 'psychological sin', that is, 'a childish weakness and love of shelter and petting, a neurotic shrinking from full human life, a morbid preoccupation with failure and guilt'. These are hymns of the 'Weary Willie' type, which she said should never be sung in congregations where the average age is less than sixty. 'Equally unsuited to general use are those expressing disillusionment, anxiety, or impotence' (LS 115). Whatever her own personal struggles, she would put a brave face on things, it seems.

Evelyn Underhill's mother died in 1924, the year in which she began to travel widely in Britain to lecture and give addresses. One invitation came to her from George Bell, then still Dean of Canterbury, to give a retreat for women in Canterbury Cathedral. She was honoured by her Fellowship at King's in 1927. And her final phase of writing directly about the Christian mystics came with a book significantly entitled *Mystics of the Church* in 1925.

Pilgrimage as an Anglican

Evelyn Underhill's memorial volume to von Hügel was published in 1927 with the title *Man and the Supernatural*. Somehow or other, by his own prayers and by what he said to her, according to her, he compelled her to experience Christ. 'It took about four months – and it was like watching the sun rise very slowly – and then suddenly one knew what it was.' This experience took time to have its impact on her, but then she found that 'more and more my whole religious life and experience seem to centre with increasing vividness on our Lord – that sort of quasi-involuntary prayer which springs up of itself at odd moments is always now directed to him.' She also wrote of an experience in which she both saw and felt 'how it actually is that we are in Christ and he in us – the interpenetrating of Spirit – and all of us merged together in him actually, and so fully described as his Body.' The importance of these experiences took time to be appreciated, not least in a form which could be communicated to others, but she could recall a sense of 'certitude' associated with them, and cited Augustine on 'the fragrance of those desirable meats', adding, 'Curious how keen all Saints are about food' (L 26–8). This gives us one indication of the time-span it took for her to work these experiences through into a text, for in her book *Abba. Meditations on the Lord's Prayer* (1940) chapter six is simply headed 'Food'. From that preoccupation of her earliest writing with the ascent of the soul to God, she now, as it were, follows Christ returning from his experience of testing in the desert to the 'homely', the life of the ordinary, in which God is to be found.

Baron von Hügel had also helped her find stability within the communion of her baptism and confirmation. She acknowledged what she owed to him, sometimes with a certain acerbity, not least to those whose decision had been to change churches.

I appreciate the superior food, etc., to be had nearer the centre of things. But the whole point to me is in the fact that our Lord has put me here, keeps on giving me more and more jobs to do for souls here, and has never given me orders to move. In fact, when I have been inclined to think of this, something has always stopped me; and if I did it, it would be purely an act of spiritual self-interest and self-will. I know what the push of God is like, and should obey it if it came – at least I trust and believe so.

It seemed to her indeed that God had given her von Hügel's 'immense and transforming help' but she hadn't yet been given other orders. 'After all he has lots of terribly hungry sheep in Wimbledon, and if it is my job to try and help them a bit it is no use saying I should rather fancy a flat in Mayfair, is it?' (L 195–6). She would not, as she put it in another letter, leave the trenches for the comfort of Barracks (L 210). This was where her own earlier experiences proved invaluable in the advice she might give to another. She knew perfectly well that frequent communion was a recent development, so its reception in one church or another simply couldn't be essential to the supernatural life. 'God will care for his own, and will make up in other ways to the really desirous what they can't at present receive through the sacramental channels of the Church.' Teaching prayer and adoration was something everyone could do, whether in their own homes or meeting in small groups, whatever the custom of the official Church (L 276). To another she wrote, 'You are now to rest quietly till God hands you out your next job. Who knows what? His unexpectedness is one of the most attractive things about him!' (L 339). Her own 'orders' in fact were to write and to teach, to do the things at which she excelled.

As an Anglican Evelyn Underhill's most significant publications were *The Golden Sequence* in 1932, *Worship* in 1936 bracketed as it were by *The School of Charity* in 1934 and *The Mystery of Sacrifice* in 1938. Earlier work, such as *Concerning the Inner Life* and *The House of the Soul*, not to mention *Mysticism* and the earlier bigger books from her pre-Anglican phase, were re-printed and re-read. There was an embarrassing wealth of perspectives to choose from, and she may have found her audiences expecting her to sound like her earlier self rather than the one she had become. One accidental achievement was that she established herself as in effect the first woman 'retreat director', and an important book arising from such work is *Abba* of 1934 revised for publication in 1940. It is unsurprising to learn that she was beginning to tire, to be ill, to need longer periods of rest, to undertake fewer engagements. In any case, the Second World War brought her to exhaustion point, as no doubt it brought all too many others. When we reach our last chapter, we will see how profoundly her attitude to war changed as she worked her way more deeply into the Christian tradition.

Evelyn Underhill suffered greatly from asthma and bronchitis in the last year of her life, and eventually died of a haemorrhage on 15 June 1941.

Dear night, I love thee. Take me by the hand,
Make thou the ferment of my thought to cease.
Teach me thy wisdom. Let me understand
Thine unstruck music. Give my soul release
From the day's glare and din.
Lift thou the latch, that I may push the gate
And let my Darling in.
He stands without, he wearies not to wait
Before my threshold till
Thou hast made all things proper to our state
And every voice is still.
Then thou and he shall enter side by side,
The banner shall be set above his bridge,
The curtains of thy splendour shall be spread
About our marriage bed. (T 67)

2

The Way of the Mystics

In the outline of Evelyn Underhill's pilgrimage some attention was given to material from her books so that we could be aware of development in the direction of her later positions. In this chapter, we return to three of her earliest but most important books, to look at them in more detail. These are *Mysticism* (1911), *Practical Mysticism* (1914) and *The Mystic Way* (1913). These books indicate her understanding of how someone makes progress to union with God, and how Christ's own life serves as a pattern for that progress.

Mysticism is the first of her major books. The Preface to the first edition of 1911 reveals an adventurous, non-specialist writer, drawing on the work of metaphysicians, psychologists, students of texts and symbolism, theologians and historians. If unacquainted with those whom she discusses, the best place to start may be the Appendix, 'since few things are more disagreeable than the constant encounter of persons to whom we have not been introduced'. There she sets out the meaning she gives to 'mysticism'. 'Broadly speaking I understand it to be the expression of the innate tendency of the human spirit towards complete harmony with the transcendental order; whatever be the theological formula under which it is understood.' She believes that in 'great mystics' this tendency would capture the whole field of their consciousness, dominate their lives, and in the experience called 'mystic union' they would achieve that harmony. And she thought that the desire to attain such union, and the movement towards it, was a genuine life process, exhibiting 'the true line of development of the highest form of human consciousness'.

Founded in Experience

In the substance of the book she then turns to aspirants to the mystical life. She thinks they deserve the same serious attention as we would give to explorers and pioneers. Their courage had yielded truth to them, and the same is true of mystics in their turn (M 4). Reviewing the philosophical options available in her day, Evelyn Underhill thinks none of them adequate either to include or to explain artistic or spiritual experience. For there are three apparently authoritative areas of perception and experience: that is, religion, pain and beauty. Religion is conceived in evolutionary terms as moving from magic to Pure Love. It is a schema with which many theologians of her day were uncomfortable. However, she is also insistent that nature cannot explain absolutely everything, and this is particularly so when she considers that 'We are hopelessly over-sensitized for the part science calls us to play' (M 19). Pain may seem to be an odd member of the trio, but for her it can speak of 'the terrible initiative caress of God'. 'Pain ... plunges like a sword through creation, leaving on the one side cringing and degraded animals and on the other side heroes and saints.' It also seems to her to be one of those facts of universal experience which are peculiarly intractable from the point of view of a merely materialistic philosophy (M 20), and beauty is viewed in similar terms. Seeing a mountain, hearing the skylark, enjoying the speedwell are inexplicable unless we realize that there is a reality here to which we respond not because we understand it but because we *must* respond. These three areas of fundamental difference between the mystics and most of us mean that they accept religion, beauty and pain as 'central for life' (M 23).

The Hunger of Love

Evelyn Underhill then invites her readers to a life of renewed vitality, with the evidence of the lives of the mystics before us, and with the fruit of their contemplation conveyed to us in however fragmentary a form (M 34). Whereas the metaphysician gets a side-long glance at 'Being', and the artist (going one better) gets a brief and dazzling vision of beauty, the mystic, she claims, gazes with confidence 'into the very eyes of the Beloved' (M 35). This is extremely important to her, for she goes on to say that 'the greatest contribution of the mystics to humanity's knowledge of the real' is that they find in 'this Absolute' a personal object of love (M 40). Since, for her, the parable of the Prodigal Son is about the history of mankind in its desire to 'return to the Father's heart' she uses this as her clue as to how the Absolute should be interpreted. The mystic does not just have an intuition of 'a remote, unchanging Somewhat calling him', but knows 'an intimate, adorable Somewhat, companioning him' (M 41).

She portrays a hungry self, hungry for knowledge *but* even more hungry for love, and suggests that it is our moments of passion, for example as lover, poet, mourner or convert, which furnish analogues for the act of concentration, of determined attention, which is essential for the mystical journey. The mystic is anything but passive. So she writes of the mystic's experience:

It is infused with burning love, for it seems to its possessors to be primarily a movement of the heart: with intellectual subtlety, for its ardour is wholly spent upon the most sublime object of thought: with unflinching will, for its adventures are undertaken in the teeth of the natural doubts, prejudices, languors and self-indulgence of man. These adventures, looked upon by those who stay at home as a form of Higher Laziness, are in reality the last and most arduous labours which the human spirit is called upon to perform. They are the only known methods by which we can come into conscious possession of all

our powers; and rising from the lower to the higher levels of con-
sciousness, become aware of that larger life in which we are
immersed, attain communion with the transcendent Personality in
Whom that life is resumed. (M 50)

The soul, indeed, is compared to the sea anemone which can open
and *know* the ocean in which she is bathed (M 51). Evelyn Underhill
realizes, however, that the persons whose experiences she trusts
sometimes exhibit symptoms of poor health as well as 'robust intelligence and marked practical or intellectual ability' (M 59), as
though their bodies were being strained by 'exalted spirit'. As
examples she mentions Catherine of Siena (the fourteenth-century
philanthropist, reformer and politician) and Catherine of Genoa
(an original theologian, and in the last quarter of the fifteenth
century the highly efficient matron of a large hospital). Both of
these women for periods of their lives were unable to eat anything
other than the consecrated Host at Holy Communion (M 59).
Though we might be sorely tempted, Evelyn Underhill is surely
right to say that just as we should not attempt to find the source of
the great mid-nineteenth-century dancer Taglioni's genius in the
symptoms of St Vitus's dance, so we shall not understand the extraordinary personalities of the mystics by reference to diseases of the
psyche. As with great artists, mathematicians and inventors, in
the mystic the strange depths of the human person are a source of
creativity, a treasure house of resources. 'Not to *know about*, but to
Be, is the mark of the real initiate' (M 72).

Wherever possible Evelyn Underhill returns to perfectly
ordinary instances of the sort of thing she wants her readers to
grasp. Perceiving transcendent reality may sound well beyond the
capacity of most of us, but when she links it to falling in love,
whether with a person, a landscape, or with 'the Holy', we can
begin to follow where she wants to take us. This is so despite the
fact that she would be the first one to agree that language is finally
inadequate to tell us about God. Yet even this inadequacy is

familiar to us from the achievements of artists of various kinds. Music (without words) is particularly important here, she claims, for it shares with great mystical literature 'the power of waking in us a response to the life-movement of the universe: brings us – we know not how – news of its exultant passions and its incomparable peace' (M 76). Mystics, like the musician, use symbol and imagery as best they can.

Evelyn Underhill insists that mysticism is 'active and practical', also roundly declaring that 'it is an organic life-process, a something which the whole self does; not something as to which its intellect holds an opinion' (M 81). Although it is 'practical' and the mystic does not neglect the 'multiplicity of the world', the mystic is, basically, single-hearted. The changeless One is her objective, and this One is 'also a living and personal Object of Love'. Union with this beloved is a form of 'enhanced life', possible only as the result of remaking the whole personal centre of a human being (M 81).

> Attraction, desire, and union as the fulfilment of desire; this is the way Life works, in the highest as in the lowest things. The mystic's outlook, indeed, is the lover's outlook. It has the same element of wildness, the same quality of selfless and quixotic devotion, the same combination of rapture and humility. This parallel is more than a pretty fancy: for mystic and lover, upon different planes, are alike responding to the call of the Spirit of Life. The language of human passion is tepid and insignificant beside the language in which the mystics try to tell the splendours of their love. They force upon the unprejudiced reader the conviction that they are dealing with an ardour far more burning for an Object far more real. (M 89)

Here Evelyn Underhill was laying the foundations for all her future thinking. It is as though she is inadvertently writing in *Mysticism* the portrait of a self deeply hungry for knowledge but above all for love. Whether or not it was going to be possible to satisfy that hunger for herself in her own life was perhaps always to be an open question.

Mystics and Their Maps

For the moment, however, we should notice the importance of what she says in chapter five of *Mysticism*, a chapter on 'Mysticism and Theology'. Here she acknowledges the dependence of mystics on their 'creeds', by which she means some form of intellectual structure which enables them to reflect on their experience. For her *any* religious system which 'fosters unearthly love is potentially a nursery for mystics', and this is as true of Islam and Judaism, Hinduism and Buddhism, as it is of Christianity. In all these traditions, the ways in which mystics think about their experiences is 'guessing aided by analogy'. The most crucial analogy is likely to be that made between self-understanding and the way a mystic thinks of God. For instance, 'since he must transcend his natural life in order to attain consciousness of God, he conceives of God as essentially transcendent to the natural world' (M 102). Like the Prodigal Son the mystic is on a journey, but 'in a land where there is no time and space, no inner and outer, up or down'. How he describes that land will be conditioned by a number of things, such as temperament, powers of observation, the metaphors he can use, and above all by his religious context. The 'journey', itself a metaphor for a particular form of experience, involves the purging and preparation of the self, to change its consciousness, to make possible its union with what it desires. Put more bluntly, the mystic 'has to find God' (M 103).

Without offering an opinion about the exclusive truth of any one system or revelation, Evelyn Underhill claims that the best map-makers have been Christian. This is because between that mysterious Absolute or Real which the mystics attempt to describe and our own conditioned selves Christianity offers a third term, a mediator. Alluding to the nativity stories of the first gospel she writes that such mediation 'was the priceless gift which the Wise Men received in return for their gold, frankincense and myrrh' (M 105). Christianity's note of close intimacy, 'of direct and personal contact with a spiritual reality given here and now', and its combination of splendour, simplicity, sacramental and transcendent things, makes it the most perfect setting for the mystical life (M 106). The unintelligible begins to become intelligible through the nativity of Christ. But he is more than a human mediator, as her reflections on the Christian doctrine of the Trinity make clear. For she believed that Christ's active spirit is to be discerned in 'the ecstatic and abounding life of the world', in what she calls 'Nature's Christliness': 'Thus in the rapturous vitality of the birds, in their splendid glancing flight: in the swelling of buds and the sacrificial beauty of the flowers: in the great and solemn rhythms of the sea – there is somewhat of Bethlehem in all these things, somewhat too of Calvary in their self-giving pains' (M 115–16). What Christ's life shows us is a divine, suffering, self-sacrificing Personality as 'the sacred hearth of a living, striving universe'. There is to be no absorption of the self in Reality which would make loving communion unintelligible. The personality must remain identifiable. Here again, we seem to find a very revealing comment about Evelyn Underhill herself, for she comments that for some, 'deliberate meditation upon the humanity of Christ, difficult and uncongenial as this concrete devotion sometimes is to the mystical temperament' is a necessity for a healthy and well-balanced inner life (M 121). Christ's life is then what she calls a Drama of Faith, and in itself shows us something of the necessary adventures of the human spirit.

Its obscure and humble birth, its education in poverty, its temptation, mortification and solitude, its 'illuminated life' of service and contemplation, the desolation of that 'dark night of the soul' in which it seems abandoned by the Divine: the painful death of the self, its resurrection to the glorified existence of the Unitive Way, its final reabsorption in its Source – all these, they say, were lived once in a supreme degree in the flesh. (M 121)

Using Maps

In her chapter on 'Mysticism and Symbolism' she explores maps for the soul's journey. What we need is good symbolism, whether verbal or non-verbal. Symbolism uses to the full the resources of beauty and passion, bringing with it hints of mystery and wonder, bewitching the mind and appealing to the desirous heart (M 126). In particular, she considers three classes of symbols, those of the pilgrim and wanderer, of the lover, and of the one who craves for inward purity and perfection. The symbol most important for her personally links up with her words about the Madonna and Child from an earlier book, when she wrote that she had found in the court of heaven 'Maternal Life enthroned, and on her knees/ The Son of God, the soul'. That identification with Christ she now describes in terms of a bride who accepts pains and duties in place of the raptures of love, and thus 'becomes a "parent" of fresh spiritual life'. The bride of God becomes the *Mater Divinae gratiae*, mother of divine grace, and mystics create spiritual families as partners and fellow labourers with divine life (M 140).

Yet almost any symbol will do to keep us going. The Magi, she reminds us, 'set out on a quest for the symbolic Blazing star which brought them, once at least, to the cradle of the Incarnate God' (M 152). The cold rationalist may not understand the importance of 'the embraces, gestures, grimaces, and other ritual acts by which we all concentrate, liberate, or express love, wrath or enthusiasm' (M 159), but 'all persons who are naturally drawn towards the ceremonial aspect of religion are acknowledging the strange power of subtle rhythms, symbolic words and movements, over the human will' (M 163). At this stage of her life, though, she doubted that such ceremonies would give human beings what they most needed. It was as though this was the way she *must* think at this stage, as a mere 'onlooker' of sacramental life. Later on, as a publicly committed communicant, the sacraments came to be for her the very means of renewed life.

Stages on the Journey

Evelyn Underhill had already given her readers much to think about, before she turned to the second half of *Mysticism*, which, we note, has the title of one of her books, 'The Mystic Way'. Map-making again, she tracks the three stages of awakening the self, each of which runs into the other two. The first stage is that of 'purgation', the pain and effort which coincides with a deepening sense of repentance. The self endures the pain and effort involved in being cleansed of what hinders its progress towards a richer existence, knowing that beyond such purgation is yet more transformation brought about by divine love. The second stage of awakening is that of 'illumination', the happiness of the experience of knowing that one is loved by God. For some, there is a further excruciating stage of killing the human instinct for personal happiness, to make final self-surrender possible. This stage is preparation for the bliss of union, with which mystics are impelled from 'spiritual marriage' to 'divine fecundity' (M 171–3). As criteria to distinguish voices and visions which 'come from God' from those which emerge from an active and rich but mercly human consciousness, she suggests that the former will be sources of helpful energy, charity and courage; the latter may well be expressive of 'little else but an exhaustion and tempo-rary lack of balance on the subject's part' (M 270).

Paying Attention, Enduring Pain and Finding Love

In the chapter on 'Recollection and Quiet' we begin to find Evelyn Underhill the later retreat director at work. Here she addresses herself to the hard work, the slow training which the life of the mystic has in common with that of the painter or the musician. All alike learn both from the past and from the present what she calls 'a peculiar attitude of the whole personality'. By this she means 'a self-forgetting attentiveness, a profound concentration, a self-merging' which she claims makes possible a real communion between seer and seen (M 300). And she begins to instruct us in the first stages of developing that quality of attentiveness. Here again we seem to be close to her own experience, for having chosen something exterior to the self to look at, she describes how the self perceives 'a strange and deepening quietness' and then, in the thing looked at, a 'heightened significance, and intensified existence'. Barriers melt between the self and its object. 'This humble receptiveness, this still and steady gazing, in which emotion, will, and thought are lost and fused, is the secret of the great contemplative on fire with love of that which he has been allowed to see' (M 302). Next she urges that we turn towards that Kingdom of God that lies within, to the unseen. At the tail-end of the chapter on 'Mysticism and Theology' she made a remark which we may read as perceptively and sharply self-critical, when she wrote of 'we poor finite slaves of our frittered emotions' (M 124). Now in the turn to the inner kingdom she comments on the way in which the normal self fritters its attentions on the 'manifold illusions of daily life' (M 307). Bringing the mind into subjection, stilling the will and the imagination, and letting the heart come to its own – these can be practised so that we clear away the rubbish heap of our surface interests and find the treasure house where, she claims, divine and human life meet (M 312).

Much the most demanding material in succeeding chapters is that on 'the dark night of the soul', the experience of destitution, the 'sorting-house' stage which distinguishes those who seek to *know* from those who are driven to *be* (M 383). This is a further stage of cleansing, not, this time, of our perceptions but of the 'very shrine of the self' (M 388). For some this means the experience of loss of the divine companion, when 'the old dear sense of intimacy and mutual love has given place to a terrible blank' (M 389). For another group the primary focus of this new pain is 'a new and dreadful kind of lucidity' about one's helpless imperfection. Often combined with this is the discovery that the very desire for and interest in the love of the divine companion has gone (M 390–1). Stagnation of emotion, of will and intelligence, the incapacity to control inclinations and thoughts, accompanied by 'overwhelming sensations of impotence and distress', may yet be succeeded by a different anguish: unsatisfied but passionate and uncontrollable longing for God (M 394). What is required is a kind of death.

> *Poverty leaps to the Cross: and finds there an utter desolation, without promise of spiritual reward. The satisfactions of the Spirit must now go the same way as the satisfactions of the senses. Even the power of voluntary sacrifice and self-discipline is taken away. A dreadful ennui, a dull helplessness, takes its place. The mystic motto,* I am nothing, I have nothing, I desire nothing, *must now express not only the detachment of the senses, but the whole being's surrender to the All.* (M 400)

No cross, no crown, as Christians sometimes say, crucifixion preceding resurrection (M 401–2). It sounds appalling, and no doubt it is, but beyond it lies the life-enhancing power of the Love of God 'once the human soul is freely opened to receive it' (M 415). And here she turns to 'deification' (being made like God). This, she carefully says, is 'a metaphor, an artistic expression which tries to hint at a transcendent fact utterly beyond the powers of human understanding, and therefore without equivalent in human speech' but which a Christian mystic justifies as a corollary of the Incarnation, or the humanizing of God (M 418–19). With a sense of personality recovered, intact, of love, action and will unimpaired, the final experience of Reality is best expressed in the language of the lover, the bonds of companionship growing in intimacy and splendour (M 426). She also speaks of 'theopathetic' life (life open to divine influence), which enables even those of great vitality, deep enthusiasms and unconquerable will to surpass themselves.

> In the fourth degree of love, the soul brings forth its children. It is the agent of a fresh outbirth of spiritual vitality into the world; the help-mate of the Transcendent Order, the mother of a spiritual progeny. The great unitive mystics are each of them the founders of spiritual families, centres wherefrom radiates new transcendental life. (M 431)

And here we arrive in the garden of 'Divine Fecundity', having withstood the tests of divine sonship, the sufferings of the cross, the darkness of the tomb. Picking up the language of the narrative of the fourth gospel (John 20: 1–18) she makes it come alive for her readers and their own lives. She encourages them to believe that, as in the encounters some disciples had with the risen Christ in the garden, so for us, in some least expected moment, with the common activities of life progressing, 'that Reality in Whom the mystics dwell slips through our closed doors, and suddenly we see It at our side'. Her readers themselves stand in the tradition of those who may be visited by that 'Reality' so long as their souls are 'alive and growing'. The mystics, she tells us, 'come back to us from an encounter with life's most august secret, as Mary came running from the tomb'. For Evelyn Underhill, it was necessary to endure cross and tomb, but with the promise of fruition (M 449–50).

> Like the story of the Cross, so too the story of man's spirit ends in a garden: in a place of birth and fruitfulness, of beautiful and natural things. Divine Fecundity is its secret: existence, not for its own sake, but for the sake of a more abundant life. It ends with the coming forth of divine humanity, never again to leave us: living in us, a pilgrim, a worker, a guest at our table, a sharer at all hazards in life. (M 450)

Mysticism in Wartime

Another related work reflects the experience of wartime. In *Practical Mysticism* she embarks on the task of commending what she argues for to those immersed in the hard practicalities of life. She wants them to see the world differently, to realize that the sea felt by the fish, the plants seen by the bee, the intricate sounds of the hedgerow as heard by the rabbit, 'the impact of light on the eager face of the primrose', the landscape as known in its vastness to the wood-louse and the ant – all these realities summon us beyond ourselves (PM 4–5). Our inheritance, she insists, is 'a world of morning-glory; where every titmouse is a celestial messenger, and every thrusting bud is charged with the full significance of life' (PM 13; and see 15). Her gentle wit beguiles her reader not indeed to the demands of the renunciation of the cloister, but at least to the demands of the concentration required on the golf course (PM 19). She utters again the summons to self-simplification, to free the self from its adjustment to 'a world of frittered values', incompatible interests, people, principles, things, ambitions and affections, tastes and prejudices (PM 24). Any focus of attention will do to begin with, so long as the practice of meditation is begun. There is a 'soul' or a personal self who meditates and can be discovered in the practice of meditation. If we can 'make this first crude distinction between appearance and reality', between the 'frittered' self and the 'soul' self, we can recognize an achievement comparable to that of a baby making its first effort to stand upright (PM 35). A salutary thought for some of her no doubt distinguished readers ! As the self is found, so the barriers between the self and other creatures gradually come down.

Look with the eye of contemplation on the most dissipated tabby of the streets, and you shall discern the celestial quality of life set like an aureole about his tattered ears, and hear in his strident mew an echo of

> *The deep enthusiastic joy,*
> *The rapture of the hallelujah sent*
> *From all that breathes and is.*

> *The sooty tree up which he scrambles to escape your earnest gaze is*
> *holy too. It contains for you the whole divine cycle of the seasons;*
> *upon the plane of quiet, its inward pulse is clearly to be heard.* (PM 59)

She wants us to see ourselves as parts of the whole in which, like
the tabby, we are also immersed, our 'arrogant personality' sunk
into the stream of life, so that our senses enable us to 'savour' the
world. 'Even "our fragmentary bodily senses" offer us a transient
sacrament' (PM 61–2). Having acquired the taste of reality, so to
speak, we will want more of it. And here, interestingly, she wants
us to go beyond the 'garden', even one inhabited by saints and
angels. She wants the freedom of the universe. 'You will not have
peace until you do away with all banks and hedges, and exchange
the garden for the wilderness that is unwalled; the wild strange
place of silence where "lovers lose themselves"' (PM 68). This
wilderness, bare of the material for image-making, is yet supreme-
ly 'homely', that is, satisfying, giving love for love.

> *And here the practical man, who has been strangely silent during the*
> *last stages of our discourse, shakes himself like a terrier which has*
> *achieved dry land again after a bath; and asks once more, with a*
> *certain explosive violence, his dear old question, 'What is the use of*
> *all this?'* (PM 92)

Evelyn Underhill's answer to him is an enlargement of our sense of
the universe, conditioned only by the perfection of our generosity,
courage and surrender – supposing ourselves to be like 'practical
man'. She uses also the image of a sheep finding herself in a position of creative responsibility, with a sense of correspondence not
only with the Shepherd, but with the world, sky, hedges, land, the

group to which we belong (PM 95). Take sides with creative spirit, she urges, 'with the higher tension, the unrelaxed effort, the passion for a better, intenser, and more significant life. The adoration to which you are vowed is not an affair of red hassocks and authorized hymn books; it is a burning and consuming fire' (PM 98). Life will yield us many sacramental images of Reality, for 'seen in the light of charity, it is far more sacred and significant than you supposed'. And we are faced with questions addressed to ourselves, 'What about *your* life? Is that a theophany too?' If it is in some sense a 'manifestation of God', we will find ourselves able to deal with the accidents, evil and sadness, cruelty, failure and degeneration of life, and its demands of loyalty, trust and self-sacrifice (PM 101-2). Briefly put, this is the case of her major book on *Mysticism*, addressed to those who can hardly ever have expected to have it addressed to them with such simplicity and attractiveness, the 'normal people' for whom she wrote this 'little book'. For those seeking a more explicitly Christian focus to their lives, she offered *The Mystic Way* (1913), to which we now turn.

Mysticism, Christ and the Mass

Unlike *Practical Mysticism*, *The Mystic Way* of the previous year had an explicitly Christian focus. In it Evelyn Underhill explores Christ's life as the foundation drama of a Christian mystic's faith. Christian mysticism appears on the human scene, she argues, with the life of its Founder, that is, with Christ himself, and its doctrines and experiences may be traced in other parts of the New Testament having once been discerned in the first three gospels.

Christ himself is firmly set within her evolutionary scheme of things, for, as we saw earlier, Evelyn Underhill is convinced that the aspiration to God which so marks out the mystic must to some extent be explicable in human terms. It cannot simply be attributed to a 'grace' or 'gift' completely set apart from what we know about biology and psychology in evolution. Rather, the action of grace is itself intrinsic to the world, for 'the spirit of love leading life to its highest expression' is continuous from the very first moment of creation until the present (MW 15). Those who read her work would already know that for her those whose lives embody creative grace were important – artists, poets, prophets, seers, all alike 'happy owners of unspoilt perceptions'. The possibilities of their lives are also ours, for if we throw away the mental blinkers which keep us focused on one narrow, useful path, our consciousness may expand, like theirs, and we too may enter into immediate communion with 'some aspect of Reality' (MW 18). Each human spirit may be touched by God, 'spurred to a new quality of attention', and in its turn respond in love, a love outgoing and fruitful, renewing the world (M 27–8). She believes that the richest layers of human nature include 'its powers of self-donation, its passion for romance, that immense spiritual fertility which has made so many of the great mystics of the West the creative centres of widening circles of life' (MW 34). The lives of the mystics are marked by living with many possibilities, following on from the renunciation of what seems to them to be inhibiting their maturity. This might include a particular job, family ties, emotional attachments – it would depend on personal circumstance. 'Something, if only a perambulator and feeding bottle, we are compelled to leave behind' (MW 36).

Considering Christ as the Pattern of the Soul's Progress

In the case of Jesus himself, Evelyn Underhill believes that there occurred a breakthrough in access to divine reality, for in him we see life 'exercising her sovereign power of spontaneous creation'. There had been some preparation for his arrival on the human scene in two contexts. The artist-seers of Judaism had proclaimed the need for regeneration, 'the breaking forth of new life upon high levels of joy' (MW 39–40). And the so-called mystery cults of the ancient world had taught their adherents dramas of rebirth and ascent to new life. Jesus of Nazareth experiences both regeneration and renewed life in his own person, and was thus 'the first person to exhibit in their wholeness the spiritual possibilities of man' (MW 43). Since Jesus was human as we are, this must mean that the new form of life he exemplifies is not restricted to those who are officially Christian. Rather, he inaugurates a particular phase of the universal struggle of aspiring humanity to deal with the conditions that hem it in, as it strives for more abundant life (MW 44). In following him, some mystics become the sorts of people who simply have to live in the cloister or as recluses, but if they are to be most Christ-like, they will sooner or later return in their generosity to the surrounding world, working in politics, leading armies or creating new religious orders and societies (MW 47).

To understand Jesus' breakthrough requires attention to the narratives of the first three gospels, and to what is there recorded of his words and deeds. Reflection on these texts should yield us sufficient understanding of the way in which his consciousness of divine sonship developed for us to learn what it is to be someone aspiring to 'total and life-enhancing surrender' to God (MW 62). So Evelyn Underhill encourages her readers to examine the gospels with 'innocence of eye', as free as we can be both of the distortions of popular religion and of biblical criticism, of which she had clearly read a great deal. Looked at afresh, she finds that the 'quality and power of *growth*' is a primary mark of the revelation they contain, and that Jesus' character represents, at the very least, 'a personality of transcendent spiritual genius' (MW 71). Whilst there was nothing like adequate materials for the construction of a biography of Jesus, the gospel texts were trustworthy enough for us to understand him, she believed. The reason for this was that the evidence about him has been preserved and set in order 'by the best of all witnesses, those who did not know the bearing of the facts which they have reported, or the significance of the sequence in which they are placed' (MW 73). In so far as they have an aim, it is to provide more interpretation than history, preparing the mind for an amazing future, rather than to focus attention on the past, however astonishing that may seem to have been. We should expect that the love and enthusiasm of the convert will blaze in the words of the gospels and illuminate the events of which they treat, so that what we read is better understood as a work of art than the analysis of phenomena by impartial observers. Coming into view already is her appreciation of Christian liturgy as itself a work of art, representing Christ to us under the inspiration of the gospels and our apprehension of them.

Baptism and Preaching

Beginning with the opening of Jesus' ministry and his baptismal experiences, she interprets Jesus' vision of the heavens opening, and of the descent of the Spirit upon him, as the flooding of his consciousness with the strange new life latent within him. He became aware at that moment of reality and of his own participation in it. In addition, in his particular case, Jesus experienced also 'a sudden and irrevocable knowledge of identity' between his soul and its Source, an identity so complete that only the human metaphor of sonship can express it (MW 81). The difference between Jesus and other mystics is thus that he enjoyed a complete harmony with God, 'a "sonship" never to be lost or broken', whereas the rest of us can make some headway towards that state only by long and sustained effort. That 'sonship' makes him unique among human beings (MW 82). Free of the sense of sin or of separation from God, Jesus nevertheless experiences solitude, mortification, the test of choice between power and love. To be 'perfect', therefore, is to have 'a deep and accurate instinct for an infinite number of possible paths on which life can move, an infinite number of possible attainments', and to have the power to choose between them:

It means high romantic qualities, daring vision, the spirit of adventure, the capacity for splendid suffering, and for enjoyments of the

> *best and deepest kind; for only those capable of Life are also capable of*
> *God, only those capable of romance are capable of holiness.* (MW 85)

Christ chose to turn his back on whatever would separate him from us, and we may learn from him that being at one with God makes it more and more possible to be at one with others. So for Evelyn Underhill, one lesson to be learned from the Christian doctrine of Incarnation is that in Jesus' life we see not 'human necessities shirked' but rather, 'human necessities fulfilled'.

When Jesus returns from the wilderness of temptation, however, whilst he spends himself in service to others he has constantly to find both time and space to renew his intimacy with God. The depth of that intimacy is shown to us in turn by his evidently 'irresistible passion for God', with his words more violent and vivid than anyone else's in his efforts to communicate to others his sense of power and newness (MW 86–90). It is from his preaching that we gain insight into a comparable process in ourselves, as resistance gives way to the inflowing tide of new life, and the 'Kingdom of God' comes to reign in us. In us as in him there is 'an inherited divine quality', merely latent to begin with, but which can be fanned into life. It can become in us the basis of all passionate seeking for God, of intimate and loving communion with God, and of final union with God (MW 95). So by his preaching alone Christ becomes a source of 'Divine Fecundity', that is to say, he wants his joy to flower in others, his new family:

> *More is demanded of them than of other men. Since they are capable*
> *of another vision, live at a higher tension, are quickened to a more*
> *intimate and impassioned love, total self-donation is asked of them;*
> *complete concentration on the new transcendent life.* (MW 99)

Respond to Christ, and the courage and endurance of the converted will be required.

Death and Regeneration

The strain on Jesus himself was immense. Evelyn Underhill ventures some perceptive comments on Christ's cleansing of the temple as showing to us the approach of spiritual night, of the mystic state of pain. For the incident in the temple seems to her in its violence and suddenness to be opposed to what Jesus generally taught. She thinks that it reveals him to us in a phase of instability, in which an 'abnormal inclination to abrupt and passionate action' shows him in a state of transition. Then she turns to his growing sense of danger, and the disillusion of his reception in Jerusalem. His disciples turn out to be weak, self-interested and disloyal, dull and hopeless in their resistance, apathetic to what he taught them of 'that new and splendid life of freedom which he knew and lived' but seemed unable to communicate to them (MW 114). And yet whilst he had to endure the loneliness and depression of breaking with all his earthly hopes, he could at the Last Supper make one final effort to impart the elusive secret of new life to them.

On that occasion, in commonplace actions and simple words, Christ knit together the material and impermanent stuff of things into union with immortal Spirit, made them indeed the actual 'body' of that Spirit. So 'to the obvious dependence of our physical life upon food was fastened the dependence of all spiritual life upon such Spirit absorbed and appropriated; upon "grace"'. Thus his words and actions also convince us of the fundamental kinship of humanity with the divine life in its inexhaustible creativity (MW 117). Beyond that meal, Christ's agony in the garden of Gethsemane and then his death represent to us the final destitution the mystic must risk if union with God is to be possible. Surrender of all hope and of all personal consciousness bring him to his cry of abandonment. That cry is also the beginning of his ascent to God.

It is the victorious announcement of a divine-human life seen clearly through the mists of bodily torment by the transfigured consciousness of Jesus: the sowing of a seed, the seeds of Divine Humanity, to be raised in incorruption to a people that shall be born. It marks the veritable establishment of the Kingdom of Reality: the 'new Way' made clear, emerging from human ruin and darkness in the hour of physical death. (MW 123)

The major question which remains to Evelyn Underhill at this point is how to make some sense of what she calls 'the great confused poem of the Resurrection', since she believes that 'the facts which lie behind that poem are crucial facts for the spirit of man' (MW 127). She is right to be sensitive to the ignorance and awe with which we approach the Resurrection, but believes that one central fact emerges with clarity:

A personal and continuous life was veritably recognized and experienced: recognized as belonging to Jesus, though raised to 'another beauty, power, glory', experienced as a vivifying force of enormous potency which played upon those still 'in the flesh'. (MW 128)

Jesus has now become in his own person what his vision has perceived to be possible, exhibiting reality by being it in his own transformed bodiliness (MW 129). Thus the eyes of love are seen again in a dew-drenched garden, at lakesides, on mountains, in meetings, at meals, 'in all the sweet and natural circumstances of daily life'. The reality of his resurrection, and his gift to us of his spirit can be experienced by us as we discover a joyful conviction of indestructible life in ourselves, a rush of renewed vitality from the depth of our personalities (MW 132).

The Drama and Art of the Mass

In turning to *The Mystic Way*, and in particular the chapter on 'The Witness of the Liturgy', we need to note that at this stage in her life Evelyn Underhill had become convinced that her ecclesiastical homecoming would eventually be in the Roman Catholic Church, but she had not as yet made the move. She attended Mass and other liturgies, but was necessarily a non-communicant. On travels abroad she had discovered the rites of the Orthodox Churches, and she had read widely and deeply in the literature of mysticism well beyond the range of the Christian tradition as well as within it. In her initial writing on the liturgy, some of the fruits of her experience and of her learning were transmitted to her readers, for she had taken immense trouble to try to understand the significance of the Mass. For two reasons she chose to concentrate in particular on the person of the celebrant. First, she sees him as the delegate and representative of all the faithful. 'Their wills are united to his, his hands and his voice are the organs of the community, each thing which he does, he does in the name of all' (MW 282). Second, and more importantly for her, the celebrant is the living image of every mystic, as first a partaker, and then a revealer of Divine Life, for as a specifically Christian rite the developed ceremony of the Church is a 'holy pantomime' of the experience of its Founder (MW 275).

From Evelyn Underhill's day to ours, there have been many changes to liturgical forms, and she knew a good deal about the origin and development of the Mass up to her own time. Despite the differences throughout the centuries her overall point is a constructive one. This is that the order of the ceremony links up our possible ascent to communion with God with the career of Jesus; that it links us with 'the cyclic movement of those spiritual seasons which condition the growth of the soul'; and finally that it links us with the fortunes of the whole Christian family (MW 277). The liturgy indeed tracks out the adventures of any one soul, but it closely associates that adventure on a daily basis with commemoration of those 'who have celebrated in their lives the difficult liturgy of love', who illustrate for the soul very many possibilities of life. In such examples psychology, history and life lived in the 'Eternal Now' all combine together (MW 279).

The first part of the Mass can be shared by everyone progressing in the Christian life being taken to the frontiers of the new world, as the celebrant comes to the altar steps, himself crossing the frontier of his normal world. Most Christian worshippers are familiar with prayers to convert the heart to God, prayers of penitence, readings from Scripture, recital of the creed and the preaching of a sermon. This forms the first part of the Mass, and from conversion to cleansing and beyond, the Mass swings between heaven-ward praise and the effort to preach what has been learned, until a moment of illumination is reached, which is of 'the glad and convinced consciousness of the spiritual world' (MW 286). The second part of the Mass, after the creed and the sermon, is for those capable of communion, renewing their sense of the need for humility and self-surrendered love. Particularly in this part of the liturgy the performance of certain actions conveys the meaning of the ceremony to us. And what is done with the bread and wine which have been offered transforms them into 'the instruments of the supreme communication of the Divine Life to men', food for the full-grown. Prayers for purification, and the act of washing his hands brings the celebrant as 'the image of the purged and surrendered soul' to the altar, begging from those present their support in the act he undertakes for them, together with the saints of humanity and with the dead. In the very consecration of the gifts of bread and wine divine union is found at the heart of sacrifice, and union with the one adored is achieved. With the dismissal from the Mass, 'the tale of transcendence is done', and the mystic is despatched back to the normal world in which she or he is destined to be light, leaven and salt (MW 299). Thus in the person of the celebrant Evelyn Underhill proposes we may follow the soul's journey to God and back again to the world (MW 299).

The Corporate Life

It is not, of course, that every celebration of the Mass will exemplify this overall pattern, if only because the very shape of the liturgy, the words used, the actions performed, and the ways in which these may or may not be related to one another may be clumsy, inappropriate and incoherent, as she was to point out in her short essay on 'The Mystic and the Corporate Life' (1915). Just as she had had to grapple with meditation on the humanity of Christ, so the mystic, and implicitly she herself had to endure what she called 'the cult' at its worst, in all 'its spiritual crudity, its innate conservatism, its primitive demands for safety and personal rewards' (EM 39). Even so, she thought, it was better to be within a Church than without it, since above all this means that one is a member of 'a social group which recognizes spiritual values, and therefore lives in an environment permeated by religious concepts'. At its extreme, the soul's progress may seem to have been given a problematic form but in such circumstances, she believes, lie many opportunities for training in humility, self-denial, obedience and suppleness, all of which may free us from arrogance and self-consciousness (EM 40–42). Better for the mystic to stay within the institution and urge it along from within, than sting it from without as if one was an 'enthusiastic spiritual mosquito' (EM 44). Mystics need the traditions of their institutions, and institutions need the power and passion of their great and loving spirits.

Without the ardent prayers of the mystics, the vivid spiritual life they lead, what would the sum of human spirituality be? How can we tell what we owe to the power which they liberate, the currents which they set up, the contacts which they make? The land they see, and which they report to us, the land towards which humanity is going. They are like the look-outs upon the cross-trees, assuring us from time to time that we are still on our course. Tear aside their peculiar power and office from the office of the whole, and you will have on one side a society deprived of the guides which God has raised up for it, and on the other an organ deprived of its real perfection and beauty, because severed from the organism which it was intended to serve. (EM 58)

Given such statements in print, how long could she remain where she had placed herself, living like a 'beginner', but longing for the life of full communion? Within some five years or so, she slipped quietly back into public commitment to the Church of England, and it was as a member of that Church that she gave her lectures in Oxford on *The Life of the Spirit and the Life of Today*, and launched herself in mid-life as an authority on religious renewal. The range of what she saw as being involved in renewal is impressive. In her introduction to the modern edition Susan Howatch, for instance, commends attention not just to Evelyn Underhill's interest in psychology, and to what we presently call 'interfaith dialogue', but to her assessment of the power and influence of suggestion, and of the importance of finding and providing a spiritual dimension to education. At this stage of her life she owed much to von Hügel for whom she wrote *Man and the Supernatural* in 1927. At this juncture, however, we need to turn to our third chapter, and to the thinking of the fully mature Evelyn Underhill in her major texts from *The Golden Sequence* of 1932 to *Abba* of 1940. It was in this phase of her life that she was to discover her sacrificial understanding of pacifism, as identification with Christ in his cry of abandonment in the hope that true life would emerge from what seemed utter disaster.

Return to the Father's Heart

Having made the move back into the Church of England, Evelyn
Underhill worked her way into a deeper appreciation of Christian
doctrine. In this chapter we see what she made of it. First we follow
her thinking in *The Golden Sequence* (1932) together with
Abba. Meditations on the Lord's Prayer (retreat addresses of 1934,
published in 1940). Just as we saw in the previous chapter that
Practical Mysticism and *The Mystic Way* were closely related
together, with the second having a sharper focus on the person of
Christ, so we will see an analogous relationship in *The Golden
Sequence* and *Abba*. In the second part of this chapter we begin
with *The School of Charity: Meditations on the Christian Creed*
(1934) which is concerned with the creed which is central to the
Christian eucharist. We then look at *Worship* (1936), the book
from the second part of her life which is comparable to *Mysticism*.
And we conclude with *The Mystery of Sacrifice: a Meditation on the
Liturgy* (1938). This book crowns and completes her chapter on
'The Witness of the Liturgy' from *The Mystic Way*. As we shall see,
in this period she came to focus more and more on the centrality
of the cross and on Christ's cry of abandonment. This focus is
central to her mature conviction that it was a vocation, at least for
some Christians, herself among them, to follow Christ in final
trust in God, believing that out of such self-giving new life might
arise. This was her image of the 'slain soul' put to the service of a
sacrificial understanding of pacifism.

Come, Thou Holy Spirit, Come

'The Golden Sequence' is the customary way of referring to the Christian hymn, *Veni Sancte Spiritus*, nowadays attributed to Archbishop Stephen Langton of Canterbury (died 1228). 'Come, Thou Holy Spirit, come' is found in translation in many standard hymn books. In writing about the Holy Spirit Evelyn Underhill was attempting to make sense of a much-neglected topic in Christian thinking, and to make sense of it in her own way. The 'Absolute' and the 'Lover' of *Mysticism* become in her reflections on *The Golden Sequence* the Spirit and the Father. But the ground-plan of *Mysticism* remains essentially intact.

In the Preface to *The Golden Sequence* she acknowledges that the 'modern soul' inherits the traditions of the past, but points out the importance of the transformation of our sense of the universe which had come about even in her own time. It was in the context of this new consciousness that intelligibility had to be given to Christian doctrines. On the other hand, some of her most deeply held convictions remained entirely firm. Thus at every opportunity she would continue to resist the collapse of adoration of God into mere altruism, and the confusion of genuine charity with merely humanitarian sentiment. Pious naturalism abounds in good works, but as she steadfastly believed, only 'eternal sources of power' produce creative sources of energy. Furthermore, whilst she recognized the emphasis in German-speaking theology of the 'otherness' of God, of the sense of divine transcendent majesty, she believed that too much stress on divine 'otherness' could bring with it 'a crushing sense of helplessness', of a completely unbridgeable gap between prayer and action, between the divine and our own lives. For her, the doctrine of the Spirit made twofold sense. First, it helped to explain the meaning of the revelation of God to us: we have to pray to God to come to us. And second, it enabled us to make sense of our capacity to respond to the divine generosity in so coming to our lives. Such response was best understood by paying attention to the practices of prayer and purification which might enable us to fulfil our destiny as spiritual beings.

Giver of all Gifts

As she understood the matter, God-Spirit transcends us, is 'over-against us', yet is intimately present with and through us (GS 5). Irresistibly attractive, Spirit as 'holy spaceless Presence' is everywhere available to us. 'The self-revelation of Spirit to its sense-conditioned creatures goes all the way from the cosmic to the homely. It can bless the votive candle, and burn in the star.' To believe this is no matter of merely 'natural religion', for the witness of the Bible is to Spirit as 'the awful intervention of the very Life of God, at once a living spring and a devouring fire' (GS 16). The Spirit in our lives compels and transforms us, uses and modifies us, overrules and energizes our clumsy lives. Spirit-filled, we may well find that life is subject to 'sudden new incitements, fresh personal lights, and calls and penetrations, the ceaseless possibility of novelty' (GS 21–2). And through Christ's own personal experience and teaching on 'our heavenly Father' we find the confidence to name God in terms of personal action, itself the outcome of a personal relationship.

To call God 'Father' is to be carried beyond the sense both of measureless reality which is 'wholly other', beyond even a sense of divine creative and fostering presence, to 'a closer link, a certain profound likeness in nature, a fetter of love' between God and ourselves. So Evelyn Underhill thought that if nature was 'like a great fresco where we see the breadth and splendour of the thought of God', our own soul could be thought of as like 'a little bit of ivory, on which the same Artist works with an intimate and detailed love' (GS 30). Reflectively self-critical, she commented: 'Talk of the "Mystic Way" and its stages or the "degree of love", may easily deceive us unless the Divine immanence, priority and freedom be ever kept in mind' (GS 49).

Creative Spirit

There was for Evelyn Underhill one powerful image of our relationship to God, recalled from one of her visits abroad:

There is on the north porch of the Cathedral of Chartres a wonderful sculpture of the creation of Adam. There we see the embryonic human creature, weak, vague, half-awakened, not quite formed, like clay on which the artist is still working: and brooding over him, with his hand on his creature's head, the strong and tender figure of the Artist-Creator. Creative Love, tranquil, cherishing, reverent of his material, in his quiet and patient method: so much more than human, yet meeting his half-made human creature on its own ground, firmly and gradually moulding it to his unseen pattern, endowing it with something of his own life.

***

The I will of an Absolute Power translated into the I Desire of an Absolute Love; awful holiness reaching out to earthly weakness, and wakening it to new possibilities. (GS 64–5)

She admitted that there was something not quite right about this image, for it failed to capture the sense in which we could be inspired to respond to the Spirit, taking our part as agents and tools of God in his redemptive action in the world (GS 69). So far, 'salvation' for her meant *our own* dedication for self-offering in response to God, abandoning safety and self-comfort:

For the flame of Living Love is not a mild and tempered radiance. It burns as we approach, and only gives us of its ardour and its glory when we dare to plunge into its very heart. Perhaps all earth's lesser demands and vocations, the sacrificial call of truth and beauty, the passion of the explorer or the mountaineer, overriding selfishness and ease, are parts of the intricate process by which souls are trained for the supreme self-giving of eternal life. (GS 76)

Ascending the Cross

Evelyn Underhill's second appeal to a work of art was to a picture showing a saint at the foot of the cross, with 'the Crucified stooping to his servant and by one arm drawing him to union with himself' (GS 97). Here was a better image of desire and grace, of the human upward struggle and the generous stooping down of the divine. The point of attempting to ascend the cross was at least to approach 'the absolute self-stripping of sanctity' (GS 99). To change from image to metaphor, she also wrote that the ascent to which we are called is that of the narrow way, of the rock, the rope and the guide. Such a stripping of preference, comfort, softness, unreality and excess will render us at last capable of what is being asked of us, whilst at the same time being made capable of receiving all that may be given to us (GS 105). As she rightly reminds us, 'Christ never represented salvation as something to be attained easily' (GS 107).

It is not that we can fully know what the ascent to the cross may finally entail, but she believes that we know at least that the cross must be taken into the most hidden sanctuary of the personality, placing ourselves without reserve into the hands of God (GS 140). And as we do so, she believes, a sympathy is set up 'between the soul and its Home and Father' (GS 171), expanding the soul to be more deeply living and creative:

> There is no test, no conflict, no attraction or delight, nor any vicissitude of circumstance which does not come to us charged with Spirit; no point in the chain of succession where the Eternal cannot be found, served and adored. And in this double status and the double demand which it makes on us, abides the tension and the richness of our mysterious life. (GS 192)

It is in her analysis of the Lord's Prayer that Evelyn Underhill develops her own perceptions of what the ascent to the cross *could* mean, by following the path of Christ, Word Incarnate, in his relationship to Abba, the Father of his soul and of ours, in this his own prayer.

Whereas in *The Golden Sequence* the matter of ascent to the cross comes in towards the end of what she wanted to say, in *Abba* it appears very early, in the second chapter. There she instructs us that to use Christ's prayer supposes and requires on our part unconditional and filial devotion to the interests of God. 'Those who use the prayer must pray from the cross' (AB 10). Devotion to God's interests must be pursued with courage, confidence and zest: 'asking, seeking and knocking with the assurance of the child, not with the desperation of the lost and starving slave'. To say 'Abba' is to believe that God showers love upon us as we shower it upon children. In that trust, everything can be offered to God in return, without stopping to count the cost (AB 27). And now she is unambiguously clear that the world is saved not by evolution, or by the aspiration of the human soul to God, but by incarnation, that is, with life-giving *incursion* into this world of the divine being, God with us. We are then to hope for 'the whole creation won from rebellion and consecrated to the creative purposes of Christ' (AB 30).

If people were unsure of how to co-operate with God at the simplest level, Evelyn Underhill urged on them direct responsibility in their use of things – money, time, position, the politics we support, the papers we read. She was wary of supposing that drastic social reform or dethronement of privilege would of themselves bring in the Kingdom, but such social policies would at least clear the ground.

The coming of the Kingdom is perpetual. Again and again freshness, novelty, power from beyond the world, break in by unexpected paths, bringing unexpected change. Those who cling to tradition and fear all

novelty in God's relation with his world deny the creative activity
of the Holy Spirit, and forget that what is now tradition was once
innovation: that the real Christian is always a revolutionary, belongs
to a new race, and has been given a new name and a new song. God is
with the future. (AB 33–4)

She fully expected the Church to exhibit evidence of renovation
from within, to escape the ever-present danger of stagnation, yet
her primary focus is not on the institution, but on the individual
person. Within the Church or without, dedication to God may
mean vigorous, self-sacrificing work. It may also mean surrender-
ing such an 'active' life for a passive life of the kind that will
give God an unhindered passage. If the final lesson of self-
abandonment is the requirement of the entire subordination of
one's own small actions and choices to God's, then what will be
asked of us is a quiet acceptance of God's firm yet gentle pressure
on our lives as he moulds us to his will (AB 45–6). And given the
course of human history, there is and always will be plenty of
scope for the acceptance of the cross in the context of cruelty,
violence and the injustice by which we conduct our affairs.

This sense of utter dependence on God does not come to us 'from
a religion of Safety First':

It is the teaching of One who knew in the wilderness the full tempta-
tion which comes with the possession of great powers, and in Gethse-
mane the awful face-to-face encounter with the forces of destruction,
the horror and trembling of spirit before approaching agony, darkness
and death. So austere, so arduous is the Christian programme, so real
the struggle and so rough the journey to which the soul is called, that
only when guided by a Spirit who knows the route better than we do,
can we hope to get through without disaster. (AB 81)

In the sacrifice of the cross Christ, the manifestation of Absolute
Beauty, the Perfect, the Strong, the Radiant, self-offered for the

sinful, the murky, the weak, achieved his victory through suffering, failure and death, but beyond it he looked to the Father whose presence is already with us and awaiting us, as Evelyn Underhill believes.

Divine Sustenance

Writing on 'Food', Evelyn Underhill explores our entire dependence on God, but does this by linking the Lord's prayer for daily bread to the eucharist. As she explains, our humbling dependence on food from beyond ourselves is the expression of a deeper mystery, of the identity of Giver and Gift. God himself is the soul's food. So praying for true bread is prayer for God's imparting of himself to us, and in the prayer God is already given, 'for the petition of the creature and the self-imparting of the Creator are one movement'. God gives without stint all that we need, but we must do our part. 'He gives the wheat: we must reap and grind and bake it. Even the eucharistic gifts must cost us trouble, bear the imprint of man's toil' (AB 52–3). The pattern of taking life and of giving life, of taking food and giving food, is our most fundamental clue to the way God gives himself to us. So the mystery of the eucharist does not stand alone, but is rather a total sacramental disclosure of the dealings of the transcendent God with us (AB 58). In the final group of books to be considered here, Evelyn Underhill focuses even more sharply on God as Giver and Gift, and on the life of the worshipping Church which sustains her. And she does so, to begin with, by attending to the creed used in the eucharist by Christians of all Churches, both west and east, the fourth-century one known as the Nicene Creed.

In the Preface to *The School of Charity: Meditations on the Christian Creed* (1934) she reminds her readers of something she herself had come most deeply to appreciate, in her movement back into the community of her baptism. This was that 'the greatest masters of the spiritual life speak to us from within the Church; accept its teachings, and are supported by its practices'. The truths of the creed which may seem all too familiar to us are in fact many-levelled, and yield richness and beauty to those who take the trouble to explore them. At this stage of her life, Evelyn Underhill turns away from what she refers to as 'foreign imports'! Attention to other religious traditions is now absent from her work.

The central conviction of her writing on mysticism is now re-affirmed, that God is Love, or rather, Charity – that is, generous, out-flowing, self-giving love. This love she now describes as the colour of the divine personality, the spectrum of Holiness. Response to this divine artist will transform our self-centred desires into 'the wide-spreading, outpouring love of the citizen of Heaven' (SC 10–11). Just as in *Mysticism* she had addressed herself to the experience of pain as the 'initiative caress of God', she turns to it again, facing more squarely the difficulty of sustaining a conviction of God's love in the very teeth of all too much evidence to the contrary. For injustice and greed, misery and failure which seem to be 'the direct result of corporate stupidity and self-love' not merely offer us all too much opportunity for the expression of disapproval and disgust. They may tempt us to despair. Nor will she now allow her own delight in the beauty of the world to let her avoid the fact that the non-human world too is shot through with suffering. 'It is easy to be both sentimental and theological over the more charming and agreeable aspects of nature. It is very dif-ficult to see its essential holiness beneath disconcerting and hostile appearance with an equable and purified sight; with some-thing of the large, disinterested Charity of God' (SC 14). But she has not lost sight of the divine caress, by any means.

For as in *The Golden Sequence* so here too she recalls us to a sense of God's 'artistry'. As a human artist may attend to a miniature two inches square as readily as to a large-scale fresco, so for her God's splendour and heart-searching beauty is truly to be discerned in his intimate and cherishing love of particular persons. 'It is an unflinching belief in this, through times of suffering and conflict, apathy and desperation, in a life filled with prosaic duties and often empty of all sense of God, that the creed demands of all who dare recite it' (SC 18). That love shown to us by God may require a particular kind of response, however.

Self-abandoned Love

It is in her meditation on the clauses of the creed which baldly recall the reality of Christ's own suffering, that Evelyn Underhill reflects further on the mystery of suffering, and how it may be changed by creative love into willing sacrifice. 'Love, after all, makes the whole difference between an execution and a martyrdom. Pain, or at least the willingness to risk pain, alone gives dignity to human love, and is the price of its creative power' (SC 55). Yet it would be as false to say of Christ's life that the whole of it was a 'cross' as it is to say that of our life. We may think that in the contrast between two phases of Christ's life she finds a means to reflect on her own, and a changing sense of her vocation in these writings in the period leading up to the Second World War. First, she recalls the deep happiness of Christ's ministry within the natural world, 'healing what is wrong in it, and using what is right in it, and sharing with simplicity the social life of men'. But then, she discerns a sense of increasing conflict with that very same world, and the growing conviction that what is so deeply wrong with it can only be mended by a love that is expressed in sacrifice (SC 56). To this sacrifice our own lives may be united in response to the summons to hallow those lives by transforming them into his. Ordinary life provides us with plenty of practice, but war now explicitly comes into the focus of her attention as a quite fundamental betrayal of trust, along with acquiescence in the second rate, and incomes drawn from dubious industries. We do not know whether she had armaments in mind. Whatever the situation, faith represents for her a demand that we face reality, with all its difficulties, opportunities and implications (SC 105).

With this persistent theme of the self-abandonment of love in mind we turn now to *Worship* (1936) and to one element in the life of prayer which Evelyn Underhill emphasizes in *The Mystery of Sacrifice* (1938). This will take us through to a new emphasis in her vocation as Europe slid once more into war. We cannot attend to every feature of *Worship*, but we need at least to see why it is still important, and still in print more than fifty years after its first publication.

Corporate Life

In the first half of her life, Evelyn Underhill had been willing to learn from religious traditions other than the Christian about the experiences of mystics. We know also that for years she regularly attended Roman Catholic services. On her travels abroad she had discovered some of the splendours of the Orthodox tradition (L 112), and back home attended the liturgies of the Russian Orthodox Church (L 249). She joined the Society of St Alban and St Sergius (the two original martyrs of the English and Russian traditions respectively). As *Worship* reveals, she had also participated as best she could in many services of a whole spectrum of denominations, whether those of a Norwegian Lutheran church tucked away in a remote valley, or of the Salvation Army in a poverty-stricken part of London. She had had long practice at a measure of participation in Christian worship where she herself was not accepted as a member of a particular communion. She had learned to look and to listen, to pray and to sing, to repeat the words of unfamiliar prayers with intelligent and imaginative sympathy. She could say with the authority born of long personal experience that we can and must learn to penetrate below the surface of any and every ritual pattern to appreciate the spiritual realities it embodies and seeks to express:

> *The Christian liturgies are the ceremonial garments worn by the*
> *Bride of Christ; garments of which every detail and ornament has or*
> *had significance as an expression of her love and adoration, or a*
> *memorial of her past, but which lose all beauty and interest when*
> *regarded apart from the life which they are intended to clothe, and the*
> *unseen realities which they are intended to suggest.* (W 187)

She invites us in reading *Worship* to realize the inheritance of the Jewish tradition which is reflected in the gospel accounts of Christ's life and in the words attributed to him. Jewish worship and belief teaches us of the divine greatness and nearness, holiness and presence. Mediation on behalf of others and moral demands flowing from worship are woven together in the psalms. And the temple liturgy of prayer, festival and sacrifice made possible the co-operation of sense and spirit, and the co-operation of all present (W 159-60). Then to synagogue worship Christians owe services centred on reading Scripture aloud, and reflection on it. She reveals her own preoccupations where she comments on the significance of sacrifice expressed in Isaac's willing acquiescence in the utmost demand of God. The traditions which developed as a result of reflection on his 'binding' as a sacrifice 'came to possess something of the devotional value which the crucifix has for Christian piety' (W 154–5).

The fruits of her exploration of the whole range of Christian worship from its earliest development are offered to her readers. We might well acknowledge her as a born ecumenist, that is, able to appreciate and love the Church worldwide, and to value the distinct and different contributions of all Christian denominations and groups, from the night-time prayers of the monk or nun to 'the Salvationist marching to drum and tambourine behind the banner of the cross' (W 53). We may imagine that although a Protestant herself as a member of the Church of England, many forms of Protestantism may have been difficult for her to appreciate, but she had had the patience to learn. And she may have learned from Protestantism something of increasing importance to her throughout her life, that is, the involvement and responsibility of the laity for the worship which was as much their responsibility as it was that of the celebrant or minister.

So in Roman Catholicism, for example, she valued 'unfastidious generosity' (W 189) towards whatever might become a vehicle of the experience of God. She herself had learned to rejoice in many different levels and strands of worship, including those of what to the fastidious might seem to be merely 'popular' religion. She would have welcomed the restoration of the eucharist as an essentially corporate act of congregational worship, but not the stripping away of many popular devotions associated with it. Then, given her *Spirit-God* devotion of *The Golden Sequence* she spotted something in common between the Eastern Orthodox tradition and the Quakers. In the Orthodox eucharist she realized the importance of the invocation of the Spirit at the moment when the bread and wine are consecrated. For their part, the Quakers had recovered a biblical sense of the 'leadings of the Spirit', thus evoking as one body of people 'a response marked by reverence, love, certitude, and above all unlimited trust' (W 234).

In the Calvinist tradition she found a restored balance between word and sacrament, with an integral connection to be made between the two, at least in her mind. For the word was indeed something objective, holy and given, but was itself a sacrament in the sense that it was the 'sensible garment in which the supra-sensible Presence is clothed' (W 211). Christians of one kind might adore God in an image, whereas others would find enrichment in chewing over the metaphors, narratives and parables of Scripture. One strength of the Reformation was the rejection of every possible substitute for 'realistic contrition and moral earnestness' (W 210), and another source of strength had come from Lutheranism. Here she valued its collection of hymns, which like the psalms had become a readily available popular prayer book. Baptists had recovered the connection between baptism and personal faith; Quakers practised together shared contemplative prayer. 'They aim at the uncompromising application of spiritual truth everywhere and at all times' (W 237). She does not explicitly mention Quaker pacifism here, and her own was nourished by the signs and symbols they insist on doing without. But she must have recognized in them what she too had learned, that whatever the final responsibility of any particular person for his or her choices, a shared life of worship and prayer was crucial to avoid delusion about what one was up to, whatever the choice made. She was right to notice that Quakerism does not entirely succeed in the total elimination of sensible signs: 'The bareness of the Meeting House is in itself sacramental; a positive witness to the otherness of God, which may be more impressive, more suggestive of the unseen Holy, than the veil before the tabernacle or the sanctuary lamp' (W 238).

In the Church of England of her own day she embraced both 'evangelical' and 'catholic', and had come to enjoy corporate parish worship and parish life in all its manifestations, such as the children's corner, the mission service, the practice of personal devotion and prayer groups, and the realistic development of fellowship. Her own all-embracing but discriminating charity is in marked contrast to partisan movements of all kinds. 'The hard, the exacting, the intolerant cannot worship; for worship is a confident approach to the Infinite Charity, and here the genial humility which realizes our common fragility and need of pardon is the only passport' (W 175).

Going into Action

In her chapter on 'Sacrament and Sacrifice' she reflects again on Christ's life, but this time believes that his life and mission are conceived by *him* from beginning to end in terms of sacrifice. By the picture language of sacrifice both he and his followers describe him, whether as at baptism by association with the dove (symbol of the Spirit), the meek offering of the poor, or with the lamb of sacrifice. His deliberately accepted death offers his life to God, and in being offered is transformed by God. By means of and through this life God enters into communion with us (W 43).

> *That humiliation of the Word which is the essential truth of Incarnation would hardly be complete enough to meet the need of His creatures, unless He were conformed to the mysterious law of sacrifice. Nor would the responsive worship of man be complete, unless there were included in it some sacrificial act or implication.* (W 45)

In *The Golden Sequence* she had written that one implication of response to Christ's sacrificial action was the practice of intercessory prayer. One who intercedes for others is deliberately vulnerable, standing in the gap between the world's needs and divine love (GS 190). And there was much to pray about:

> *It is clear, for instance, that the fervent and competing supplications born of national or sectarian intolerance, which demand with complete assurance the failure or success of military operations, the triumph of opposite doctrinal views, or the conversion of individuals from or to a particular Christian Church, cannot all be the work of the Spirit Who 'prays in us and above us'.* (GS 181)

To this work of intercession she gives a short chapter in *The Mystery of Sacrifice*, relating to those intercessions customarily placed at the very heart of the Christian eucharist. Intercession is an activity of the Christian's family life, embracing the apparently hopeless and disgraceful, the horrors, and the failures, final disillusionment and loneliness (MS 33–4). One of the most helpful features of this little book is her own choice of prayers from ancient liturgies, and those selected for the chapter on intercession include the following petitions:

Destroy wars and battles from the ends of the earth, and disperse all those that delight in war; and by thy divine mercy pacify the Church and the Kingdom, that we may have a safe habitation in all soberness and piety.

***

Remember, O Lord, Christians travelling by land or sea, those in foreign lands, those in bonds and in prison, those in captivity, in exile, in mines, and in torture and bitter slavery, our fathers and brethren.

***

Remember, Lord, all men for good: Master have pity on all; be reconciled to us all; make thy many peoples to live in peace. Scatter hindrances; bring wars to an end; make the divisions of the churches and the uprisings of heresy to cease. Undo the wanton insolence of the nations. Give us thy peace and thy love, O God our Saviour, the hope of all the ends of the earth. (MS 37)

These prayers, she knew, could not be sustained without recovering a re-orientation to the future of what she believed would be a transfigured world beyond war. Long ago, she had written to a correspondent that 'People seem often to forget that Hope is a cardinal virtue necessary to salvation like Faith and Love: an active principle which ought to dominate life' (L 66). Then in writing of the coming of the Kingdom in *Abba* she had written of hope, in much the same invigorating style in which she had written of the energies of the life of prayer at the beginning of the First World War.

The supernatural virtue of hope blesses and supports every experiment made for the glory of his Name and the good of souls: and even when violence and horror seem about to overwhelm us, discerns the secret movement of the Spirit inciting to sacrifice and preparing new triumphs for the Will. (AB 34)

Evelyn Underhill had already found an image of hope in the small birds she so much loved. Long ago, in *Immanence* she had a poem about a tiny bird finding its way into an abbey during the eucharist, and how its singing had brought the whole countryside to mind and imagination (I 24–5). Now for her hope could be found in the life of autumn migrants, turning from land, food, shelter, and a certain measure of security to fly across oceans, destitute of everything they needed. 'Perhaps some day men will rival the adventurous hope of the willow wren and the chiff-chaff: an ounce and a half of living courage, launching out with an amazing confidence to a prospect of storms, hardship, exhaustion – perhaps starvation and death.' She understood why Christ found significance in their life, and in her turn, she thought that hope had as it were been tried out in the birds.

Long ages before we appeared, the clouds of tiny migrants swept over the face of this planet. Incarnate scraps of hope, courage and determination, they were ready at a given moment to leave all and follow the inward voice: obeying the instinct that called them in the teeth of peril and diffi- culty, giving themselves trustfully to the supporting air. (HS 135–6)

So this time round, her response to wartime was different. For one thing, bombing from the air precipitated evacuation of children to the countryside, if not of whole families. Those who returned slept in their cellars, if they were fortunate, and in shelters or the Under- ground if they were not. The crisis for her was now such that only the deepest understanding and most heroic and other-worldly acceptance of the cross could resolve (L 283). In the months before her death she was more and more sure that Christianity and war were incompatible, but acknowledged that for some war was one of the two ways in which Hitler must be resisted. For only a very

few (like the birds) were ready for 'loving and unresisting abandonment to the worst that may come' without forcing this on to others
(L 308). She had prepared some Christians for the 'night-shift' (FS 16)
and taught a prayer group she had formed that it was one of their
great duties to pray for their enemies. Christians offer themselves to
God, 'to do what He asks and bear whatever He calls us to bear.
There is and will be suffering for all of us. There are only two ways of
taking suffering. We can resist and hate it, or we can accept it as a
privilege and thank God for it' (FS 55–6).

> We should not forget that as Christians we are specially bound to pray
> for our enemies: not only for the innocent people of Germany, but also
> for those who have brought this evil and misery on the world. We
> should ask God to have compassion on their sins and mistakes and
> support them in their sufferings: to save us from the spirit of hatred
> and bitterness and bring us to a just and lasting peace. We should pray
> for all children, in whom hope of the future rests. (FS 47)

She had rediscovered hope, and found a way of practising love in
the teaching of peace, recalling that it was when he drew nearest
to the crisis and final agony of his life that Christ emphasized it
more and more, knowing that this meant anything but apathy.
Peace can co-exist with 'the sharpest pain, the utmost bewilder-
ment, the agony of compassion which feels the whole awful
weight of evil and suffering' linked with altar and cross (FS 13).

The peace that Christ taught the nearer he came to the end of
his own life was the peace she now sought, the peace of absolute
acceptance, utter abandonment to God, a peace inseparable from
sacrifice. 'The true pacifist is a redeemer, and must accept with joy
the redeemer's lot. He too is self-ordered, without conditions, for
the peace of the world' (MG 201–2). As it happened, by dying in
June 1941, she herself was spared the full burden of knowledge of
what was to come in mainland Europe and far beyond it, but her
demanding legacy remains with us.

4

Conclusion

Evelyn Underhill's own life raises certain questions for us. We do not know much about her motivation and commitments apart from what she reveals in her published writing, and, more recently, in her notebooks, letters and other material combed over by editors of her work. But her biography is interesting in that it raises a question about why it was that she did not formally rejoin the Church of England until she had established for herself an independent and authoritative voice of her own. How are women to find a public role within the Christian Church and what is that role to be? If they are so gifted, how do they find a teaching role within the Church? And inside and outside the Church, what contribution, and in what way, may and do women work as theologians? Is Evelyn Underhill an example of a creative and courageous boundary pusher for other women, if they need such examples?

Another set of issues has to do with how someone finds a religious vocation within a specific Christian denomination. Will that denomination sustain growth and change in a particular person? What makes people want or need to change from one denomination to another? Ought they always to make the move, in any case?

Then there are topics in her published works to which we have only been able to allude. For instance, how important is it that there should be a spiritual dimension to education? And does it matter whether or not those who teach religion to others in an educational institution should actually be engaged in the worship and prayer life of a religious tradition, inhabiting it from the inside, so to speak? Can religion be effectively taught unless its teachers are in active engagement with a religious tradition, being transformed by it life-long?

Unless we assume that religion ought to be eliminated from life, but is rather crucial for the living of a life, on what resources do we need to draw to appreciate it? What is the role of our innumerable art forms in religion? How important is the enjoyment of so-called 'popular religion', and how crucial is it that everyone in a particular church should enjoy the whole range of possible religious expression? How free do people need to be from clerical control of or influence over popular devotions?

If we turn to mysticism, one of her life-long preoccupations, is it best understood in a cross-cultural way? If so, do mystical experiences help to establish the case for religious belief? Does mystical experience help to authenticate a religious tradition? Is it more or less important, for instance, than an appeal to the past, to history? Or is it one of the ways in which that past can be made to come alive for us? And what do the mystics have to teach us of language and symbol about God? God may not be located as an object among objects, or as a person among persons, but does this mean that no particular ways of addressing God are, so to speak, sacrosanct? How are we to think of the relationship between God's mediation of himself in word and sacrament? Are both of these ultimately dispensable?

If Evelyn Underhill is right, and mystics are at least sometimes people of great energy and practicality, why do we not find more people engaging in the practice of prayer? Or is this to reduce religion to one of the functions of the human psyche? How much can we learn from the human sciences and from the course of evolution about that psyche? Evelyn Underhill much disliked a determination to 'get something out of religion'. How do we re-learn the point that spirituality is not primarily a matter of self-discovery, but of discovery of God and of the possibilities of being creative for others? In a 'quick-fix' culture, how do we practise the long-term and sustained disciplines of prayer? How much are we willing to give up in order to arrive at the kind of life that matters?

And how much are we perplexed by theologies which tell us that God is so 'other' than us, and that we are so helpless, that it is a mistake even to long for the possibility of co-operation with God? Can we really believe that the adoration of God is to have absolute and unconditional priority in our lives, and that as a result all else will fall into place?

Within the churches, how do we come to value the differences between us, rather than homogenize them out of existence? How do the laity recognize their responsibility for the life of their worshipping communities? Is liturgy the place where we learn who and what Christ could mean? Must we centre so much on the eucharist? Is 'sacrifice' much too problematic a concept for us to be able to live out?

And last, but by no means least, how do we close the disastrous gap between liturgy, theology, spirituality, natural, social and political realities? How do we learn and sustain hope for the future? And when we think of the end of Evelyn Underhill's life, she provokes us to ask about the importance of identifying moments of resistance and dissent in life, such as, for instance, pacifism under the assaults of war. To what kind of community does a pacifist need to belong? And is pacifism an inevitable result of commitment to the Christian tradition?

Readers may discover other questions for themselves even in this brief account of Evelyn Underhill's life and thought. On the other hand, ideas do not float free of human reality, and our world is in some respects so very different from hers that her preoccupations may not all be ours. But the continued publication of her books for a wide audience suggests that her voice still speaks to us through her texts. And in a century when women are discovering and rediscovering their contribution to theology, Evelyn Underhill is certainly someone who deserves recognition as a pioneering figure for them in both this and the next century.

Suggested Further Reading

Books by Evelyn Underhill

Abba. Meditations on the Lord's Prayer, Longmans, Green, 1940.

Concerning the Inner Life and *The House of the Soul*, Methuen, 1947.

The Essentials of Mysticism and Other Essays, One World, 1996.

Eucharistic Prayers from the Ancient Liturgies, Longmans, Green, 1939.

The Fruits of the Spirit, Longmans, 1952.

The Golden Sequence, Methuen, 1932.

Immanence. A Book of Verses, Dent, 1914.

The Life of the Spirit and the Life of Today, Methuen, 1994.

Man and the Supernatural, Methuen, 1927.

Mixed Pasture, Methuen, 1933.

Mysticism, Methuen, 1960.

Mystics of the Church, Clarke, 1975.

The Mystic Way, Ariel, 1992.

Practical Mysticism, Eagle, 1991.

The School of Charity and *The Mystery of Sacrifice*, Longmans, Green, 1956.

The Spiritual Life, One World, 1993.

Worship, Eagle, 1991.

Collections of Evelyn Underhill's Writings

Barkway, Lumsden and Menzies, Lucy, eds, *An Anthology of the Love of God*, Mowbrays, 1953. Includes the quotation from *Theophanies* in this present book.

Blanch, Brenda and Stuart, eds, *Heaven a Dance. An Evelyn Underhill Anthology*, SPCK 1992.

Brame, Grace Adolphsen, ed., *The Ways of the Spirit*, Crossroad, 1990.

Greene, Dana, ed., *Fragments from an Inner Life. The Notebooks of Evelyn Underhill*, Morehouse, 1993.

Greene, Dana, ed., *Evelyn Underhill. Modern Guide to the Ancient Quest for the Holy*, State University of New York, 1988.

Menzies, Lucy, ed., *Collected Papers of Evelyn Underhill*, Longmans, Green, 1946.

Williams, Charles, ed., *The Letters of Evelyn Underhill*, Longmans, Green, 1945.

Biographies of Evelyn Underhill

Armstrong, C.J.R., *Evelyn Underhill (1875–1941). An Introduction to her Life and Writings*, Mowbrays, 1975.

Greene, Dana, *Evelyn Underhill. Artist of the Infinite Life*, Mowbrays, 1991.

Index

abandonment 34, 39, 41, 47, 58
Aberdeen University 2
Adam 44
Arc, Joan of 8

Baptist Church 53
Bell, George 11
Benson, Robert Hugh 3
Booth, General 11
Buddhism 20
Butler, Cuthbert 7

Calvinist Church 53
Catherine of Genoa 18
Catherine of Siena 18
Chapman, John 3, 7
charity 23, 29, 42, 48–9, 54
Christ 6–15, 21, 29–34, 45, 54,
 57
communion 13, 18, 33–6, 55
corporate life 38
creed 20, 41, 48, 50
cross 25–6, 45–7
Divine Fecundity 23, 26, 33

eucharist 48, 53, 55

Father, God as 17, 42–3, 45–6
First World War 7–9, 56
food 12, 34, 37, 48
Frere, Walter Howard 3

Hinduism 20
hope 34, 56–8
Howatch, Susan 39

illumination 23
incarnation 25, 33, 46
intercession 55
Isaac 52
Islam 20

Jesus 30–36
John the Baptist 9
Judaism 20, 30, 52

Kingdom of God 24, 33, 46, 56
King's College, London 2, 11

Langton, Stephen 42
liturgy 36–8, 41, 61
Lord's Prayer 12, 41, 46
love 5, 16–19, 23–8, 32–7, 44,
 49–50

Lutheran Church 51, 53

Madonna and Child 5, 22
magi 21–2
Mass 29, 36–8
modernism 4
Moore, Hubert Stuart 1, 3–4

Nightingale, Florence 8

Orthodox Church 4, 36, 53
Oxford University 10, 39

pacifism 8, 39–41, 54, 61
pain 16, 21–5, 34, 49
peace 56, 58
prayer 10, 13, 38, 42–3, 48, 51,
    58, 60–1
Purgation 23

Quakerism 53–4

Reformed Church 53
resurrection 25–6, 35
Roman Catholic Church xi, 3–4,
    36, 51, 53

sacrifice 29, 37–9, 44, 47, 50,
    54, 61
salvation 44–6
Salvation Army 11, 51, 52
Second World War 8, 14, 50, 57–8
self 5–6, 21, 24, 27
Society of St Alban and St Sergius
    51
soul 4–5, 12, 18, 21–4, 27,
    36–8, 41–2, 46–8

spirit 19, 25, 29–30, 32, 34,
    42–5, 47–53, 55
symbolism 6, 19, 22

Thérèse of Lisieux 8
trinity 21

union 15, 19, 23, 34, 37

von Hügel, Friedrich 3, 7, 11–13,
    39

Ward, Reginald Somerset 3
word and sacrament 53
works, Evelyn Underhill's
    Abba 12–13, 39–40, 56
    Concerning the Inner Life 13
    Essentials of Mysticism 38–9
    Fruits of the Spirit 58
    Golden Sequence 13, 39–40, 49,
        55
    House of the Soul 13, 57
    Immanence 5, 57
    Life of the Spirit and the Life of
        Today 10–11, 39
    Man and the Supernatural 11,
        39
    Mystery of Sacrifice 13, 51, 55
    Mysticism 3–7, 13, 15–26, 29
    Mystics of the Church 11
    Mystic Way 7, 9, 15, 23, 36–8,
        43
    Practical Mysticism 8–9, 15,
        27–9
    School of Charity 13, 41, 48
    Theophanies 14
    Worship 13, 41, 51–5